STRESS THAT MOTIVATES
Self-Talk Secrets for Success

Dru Scott, Ph.D.

A FIFTY-MINUTE™ SERIES BOOK

CRISP PUBLICATIONS, INC.
Menlo Park, California

STRESS THAT MOTIVATES
Self-Talk Secrets for Success

Dru Scott, Ph.D.

CREDITS:
Editor: **Beverly M. Manber**
Designer: **Carol Harris**
Typesetting: **ExecuStaff**
Artwork: **Ralph Mapson**
Cover Design: **Martin Rollinson**

Copyright © 1992 Dru Scott, Ph.D.
Printed in the United States of America by Bawden Printing Company.

Distribution to the U.S. Trade:

National Book Network, Inc.
4720 Boston Way
Lanham, MD 20706
1-800-462-6420

Distribution to the Canadian Trade:

Raincoast Books
8680 Cambie Street
Vancouver, B.C.
V6P 6M9
604-323-7100
800-663-5714

Library of Congress Catalog Card Number 91-77750
Scott, Dru
Stress That Motivates
ISBN 1-56052-150-3

This book is printed on recyclable paper with soy ink.

PRINTED WITH SOY INK

Congratulations

Building on successes

The fact that you are reading this book tells you one of two things:

- ✔ If someone bought this book and gave it to you, it shows that someone believes in you and wants you to get even more from life.

- ✔ If you bought this book for yourself, it shows that you are not content with the status quo. You want continous improvement for yourself and your organization.

In either case, you are moving ahead with each line you read and with each exercise you explore. You are taking positive steps toward enriching your life—on the job and at home.

Dru Scott, Ph.D.
San Francisco

i

ABOUT THIS BOOK

As I've talked with clients and friends over the years, they've asked me, "When are you going to write a book on that reinforcement system you use?" With a sense of excitement, I can give a resounding, "Now!"

I feel a special passion for this material because it has helped so many people over the years. I've had the privilege of assisting thousands of people, and they have used the system to gain inspiring results.

The system does work, and it is fun, interesting and practical.

My biggest challenge in using the system arrived when I got married at age 45 to a widower with three teenage children. I learned the meaning of stress in a new way. A friend had told me that marriage is God's cure for rigidity and self-centeredness. She was right. I needed to make some major changes in myself. (At the beginning, I was convinced that *they* needed to make all the changes.)

Although I had used the self-talk system for work accomplishments, I found a dozen new applications in my personal life. The system helped me change my attitude.

I can now say with new fervency, the system does work, and it is fun, interesting and practical.

Dru Scott, Ph.D.
San Francisco

About the Author

Dru Scott is an internationally known author and seminar speaker. Her five books and six films are used around the world. Many of the principles in this book were researched and funded as part of her work with DuPont.

CONTENTS

CONTENTS (continued)

SECTION

1

The Big Connection Between Stress, Motivation and Self-Talk

❝While we cannot direct the wind,

we can adjust the sails.❞

—author unknown

SUCCESS SECRET

Most people have never been told
how big
the connection is between
stress, motivation and self-talk.

EMPOWERMENT OR STRESS— TWO VIEWPOINTS

"Empowerment is what *they* call it. Well, stress is what *I* call it," announced Brad to the seminar group around his table. He tilted his chair back and crossed his arms over his chest, "They keep wanting us to do more, and I keep saying that I have too much to do already. I can't do everything. I don't know how they expect us to do all this. You should see the things they are piling on us. On top of all that, they want us to do management's job. No wonder everybody around here is ready to file a claim for stress."

You may have heard comments like this yourself. Such comments expose the magnitude of the problems we are facing.

Exercise: Pick the Best Answer

A. I know what Brad is talking about. I see the same things going on.

B. Brad is crying "stress" when he is just trying to get out of work.

C. Brad does not have the skills he needs to be successful in today's competitive world.

D. When it comes to stress, we need to borrow the W. Edwards Deming Thirteenth Point: "Institute a vigorous program of education and training."

E. Other: _____

Whatever your choice, the problem is clear.

These challenges impact us all:

- People today are feeling stress at unprecedented levels.

- The need for realistic education and training about stress is more important than ever before.

- Today's global economy calls for each person at every level to be informed, motivated and working for continuous improvement.

HOW THIS BOOK CAN ASSIST YOU AND YOUR ORGANIZATION

This book faces these challenges with realism and practicality. Through the concepts, case stories and exercises you will discover throughout this book, you will increase your personal ability to:

- Reduce harmful stress

- Feel more energized

- Accomplish the right things at the right time

- Change more effectively and more easily

Best of all, you will learn how to put stress to work for you, master it and keep it in its place. You will explore ways to manage stress so that it clears rather than clouds your thinking; so that it thrusts you forward rather than holding you back.

As part of moving forward, now is a good time to look at the central ideas that power this book.

STRESS THAT MOTIVATES

BOOK OVERVIEW

Stress That Motivates

If a change or demand confronts us,
and we deny it or do nothing,
　　we have stress that damages.

However, when we respond
to a change or demand
by taking purposeful action,
　　we have *stress that motivates*.

This *purposeful action for improvement*
can be toward
　　• a total solution or
　　• simply containment and mastery.
(Even if our action does not totally solve the
situation, it helps us feel better and work better.)

The secret to training ourselves
to take this action consistently is:
　　positive, purposeful self-talk.

A STRESS AND SELF-TALK SUCCESS STORY

Meet Anne—a real person who puts these ideas to work. Perhaps you will see some of Anne's successes in yourself or in someone with whom you work.

Anne stood in front of the conference room, clad in a uniform of orange shirt and slacks. Lettered over the pocket of her shirt were the words "Central Sanitary District." As you listen, you can see Anne has racked up a lot of mileage over some very rough roads in life. When she begins to talk, you immediately respect her. Clearly, she is a woman who has practiced the skill of purposeful, motivational self-talk.

Sweeping the room with dircet eye contact, she says, "My success story has to include community service agencies. They helped me get sober and off drugs six years ago. I don't know what I would have done back then without the crisis nursery for my three kids."

"But I'm really talkin' about success today. I'm proud of my job with Central San. It pays a good living for me and my family. But it's sure not easy working on sewers. And every day it motivates me to do a good job so I can get a better job. But, guys, I have learned to tell myself over and over, 'One day at a time.' And when I get sick of wearing this orange uniform, I tell myself, 'It's a great uniform in October!' "

Anne's choice to use motivational rather than stressful self-talk helps her get through each day working on sewers. It is a tough job, and her job is only one of many stresses in her life. Yet her attitude is positive, her motivation is high, her spirit is inspiring.

Anne is living proof that stress does not have to defeat us. In fact, we can actually harness stress and make it work *for* us! To do that, let's touch on how stress operates and why we hear so much about it today.

CHANGE, DEMANDS AND STRESS

Hans Selye, M.D. defines stress as ''the nonspecific response of the body to any demand made upon it.'' This classic definition in *Stress without Distress* spotlights change and the demands it makes on people to adapt. Since change is closely linked with stress, let's continue by looking at changes confronting us.

The Sources of Stress Abound

Bankruptcies. Mergers. Debt. Each week headlines scream about massive layoffs and plant closures. Companies that were once household names have become as extinct as the dinosaurs. Change is all around us. That means invitations to stress are all around us. Tools for managing stress have never been more urgently needed than right now. Surviving in the stressful environment of the nineties calls for knowing how to respond to stress effectively and how to transform stress into motivation. This is true for individuals and for organizations.

The Growing Need for Motivation

Competition *is* fierce. The global economy is zigzagging on an uncharted course. The job market looks like a high-stakes game of musical chairs. People wonder where they will be when the music stops. Whether people own the company or work in the mail room, their future depends on their ability to create value, deliver quality and build a reputation for excellence. As Peter F. Drucker emphasizes in *Managing for the Future*, ''businesses will undergo more and more radical restructuring in the 1990s than at any time since the modern corporate organization first evolved in the 1920s.'' These demands and changes add up to each of us having a greater need to keep our own *motivation* high.

People who are highly motivated keep customers satisfied. They are better team members. They feel more powerful. They are also happier, more satisfied people themselves. They know that a high motivation level gives them the mental and emotional power to punch their way through times of stress.

STRESS—A CLOSER LOOK

For a popular definition, think of stress as those forces that hinder people from moving in their chosen directions. Many people regard stress as draining and deflecting and motivation as leading and lifting.

For a more specific definition, consider Dr. Selye's approach more closely. Stress is: ''the nonspecific response of the body to any demand made upon it.'' Demands can be pleasant or unpleasant. In either case, they represent demands. And demands for change add up.

What complicates the situation is that few people have been taught to believe that they can always face a demand and take purposeful action and make some improvement. If they believe, ''There is nothing I can do,'' they become mired in the quicksand of nonspecific responses. Few people have been taught the damaging implications of this belief.

Stress and Belief Systems

''Most stress is caused by our belief systems,'' says Paul ware, M.D. He is an outstanding teacher of behavioral medicine, a psychoanalyst and neurologist at Louisiana State University and the head of a psychiatric clinic in Shreveport, Louisiana. Dr. Ware continues, ''Our choices and the ways we perceive and react to life experiences cause the bulk of our stress. So much of stress has to do with people's belief systems. And we *can* change our belief systems. The person who learned early in life to think, 'I can solve problems,' or 'I can figure things out' has less stress than most people. The person who didn't learn this belief as a child can learn it as an adult.''

''When people are feeling stress they need to hear healing beliefs. When I deal with people undergoing stress, I encourage them to remember, 'You can take care of yourself. You can stay aware of your own needs and wants and take care of them in positive ways. You can get information and make good decisions. You know more about you than anyone else. You have solved problems in the past, and you can solve them now.''''

Our belief systems do influence our stress—and our motivation.

MOTIVATION AND SELF-EMPOWERMENT

Some people believe that *motivation* means enthusiasm or happiness. However, when we talk about motivation in this book, we are talking about something specific and dynamic, a driving force that draws us toward achievement and fulfillment.

Motivation is the quality of having a motive or incentive that stirs us to action toward our dreams and objectives. The mind of a motivated person is filled with targets, objectives and pictures of excellence. The motivated person pictures his or her destination. Motivation means knowing where you and your organization want to go—and having the will and perseverance to get there.

Motivation propels us toward our objectives. Stress hinders us from reaching our goals—unless we respond with purposeful action.

Mental Background Music *Self talk*

The key to overcoming stress and staying motivated is a tool called Self-Talk. Self-talk helps us bridge the gap between knowing the right things and doing the right things consistently. Simply defined, self-talk is what we repeat to ourselves—our mental background music. Most of us are not even conscious of our self-talk, yet it has a powerful influence on our stress, motivation and actions. Since we are talking to ourselves all the time, why not make our self-talk enjoyable and effective.

Your background music sounds its tone and sends its influence into the priorities and pressures you face each day.

YOUR PRIORITIES AND PRESSURES

You will gain powerful new insights from every exercise in this book. The exercise below presents a list of issues you may be grappling with right now. You will want to refer to this list later, so take a few moments now and check the issues you currently face in your personal and professional life:

☐ Reducing stress

☐ Building motivation

☐ Catching up

☐ Handling negative people

☑ Taming procrastination

☐ Communicating a picture of where you want to go

☐ Learning new skills

☐ Keeping up an energetic attitude

☐ Taking care of your own needs and wants in constructive ways

☐ Dealing with rejection

☐ Getting organized

☐ Learning new habits

☐ Listening more effectively

☐ Breaking bad habits

☐ Gaining more self-discipline

☐ Learning new skills more rapidly

☐ Implementing plans more effectively

Keep your selections in mind as you explore this book. Let your checked items be a mental magnet, drawing your thinking to practical ideas that will help you achieve what you want.

The next exercise gives you a chance to probe into on-the-job and personal situations you want to improve.

Exercise: Two Situations You Want to Improve

To help you enjoy greater benefits from this book, think about two specific situations where you want to reduce stress and build motivation. Pick one from your job and one from your personal life.

Here are some questions to stimulate your thinking about the situation you selected. Write a few notes to help clarify your thinking.

	On the job	Personal
Who is involved?		
How do you feel about the situations?		
What do you want to happen?		
What benefits do you want to gain?		
What challenges do you face in bringing about what you want to happen?		

As you read this book and do the exercises, remember the situations and the issues you checked. You will pick up valuable insights throughout this book that will help you move where you want to go.

SPEEDING UP THE IMPROVEMENTS YOU WANT

The following diagram will help you visualize the role of self-talk in determining your levels of motivation and stress. It is actually a type of flow chart depicting the process by which we experience external events and distill them into internal feelings of stress or motivation.

The Big Connection: Stress, Motivation and Self-Talk

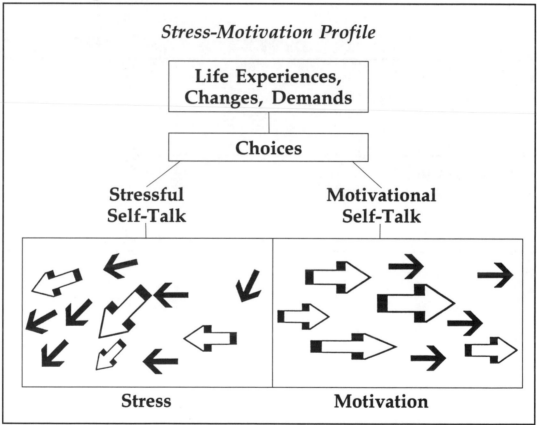

Stress-Motivation Profile

Life Experiences, Changes, Demands

Choices

Stressful Self-Talk   **Motivational Self-Talk**

Stress   **Motivation**

At the top of the chart are life experiences—those events, good or bad, pleasant or unpleasant—that we all encounter. We process those experiences by making *choices*. Psychiatrist Frank Minirth, co-founder of the Minirth-Meier Clinic, says, "Choices are the hinges of destiny." The point of *choice* is where our pathway branches either toward greater stress *or* greater motivation. The determining factor is the kind of self-talk we choose. We can describe any life experience as either a disaster or a challenge, an intrusion or an opportunity, a roadblock or a problem to be solved. We can either say, "There is nothing I can do" or "There is always something I can do."

WHAT WE SAY MAKES THE DIFFERENCE: THE STORY OF MARK

Whatever experiences life throws at us, we always have the power to choose our self-talk. Most of us know this intuitively; but when confronted with a crisis or a frustration, we often forget that the most powerful place to begin is with our self-talk. The importance of self-talk shows up in the following case.

Mark is a vice president of a Fortune 500 company. He is distinguished looking and speaks and carries himself with confidence and authority. On first meeting him, you would find it hard to believe the personal obstacles he has overcome.

He told the other people around his table, "I remember being seven years old and standing at the front door of our house. I was thinking about my family—two alcoholic parents and my seven brothers and sisters. As I stood outside the door, about to turn the knob and walk inside, I heard the voices of my mom and dad inside—loud, hostile, raised in argument. I turned and walked back to the steps and sat down. I thought, 'I am never, ever going to have that kind of life when I grow up.'"

"I didn't know what I wanted, but I knew what I did not want. I remember saying to myself, 'I'm going to work really hard so that I never have to live like that.' And I kept saying that to myself, right through high school, college and my first job. And here I am today: good family, best job in the company."

Mark is living proof that what you say to yourself makes a difference.

Exercise: Your Motivational Self-Talk Success Story

It works best to do this exercise with a partner, so ask someone at work or at home to do this with you.

How has the concept of experiences, choices and motivational self-talk worked in your own life? Remembering how the diagram flows, think of a choice you made at some time that included motivational self-talk.

1. How would you describe the life experience you selected?

_____

2. What was the choice you made?

_____

3. Your motivational self-talk: What did you say to yourself that helped you take the right action?

_____

FOR FASTER IMPROVEMENTS

You enjoy faster and greater improvements in life when you live by these life-changing realities:

- We have the power to choose how we define every life experience.

- The way we define our life experiences is revealed in how we talk to ourselves about those experiences.

- Some self-talk leads to stress: drained energy, chaotic thinking, indecision, lack of resolution.

- Other self-talk leads to motivation: incentive, direction, purpose, problem solving, problem prevention, positive action toward achieving your desired results and dreams.

The Bottom-Line Reality

While people cannot control every life experience, they can control what they say to themselves about the experience.

> ''Few people are told how much impact what they say to themselves has on how much stress they feel. What people say to themselves about an experience, their self-talk, often has more impact on their lives than the experience itself,'' says Paul D. Ware, M.D.

BUT WHAT ABOUT . . .

As you read this section, you may have experienced an inner tug. You may have felt one or more of the following responses bubbling up into your mind about your situation:

My situation is different.

There's nothing I can do.

It will never work.

I don't have time.

I tried it once, and it didn't work.

It's not that easy.

There is too much to do.

You don't know the people I work with.

It doesn't feel natural.

I know this already.

In the next section, we will look closely at these responses. Meanwhile, do not be concerned if you identify with some of these statements. People may feel that way at first. And do not be surprised if, by the time you finish reading this book, doing the exercises and putting the principles into practice, you feel the best ever with new spirit and attitude!

When you think about spirit and attitude, the next idea is a good one to keep in hand.

"I AM IN THE HOUSE AND I HAVE THE KEY"

choice

Charles Fletcher Lummis once said, "I am bigger than anything that can happen to me. All these things—sorrow, misfortune and suffering—are outside my door. I am in the house and I have the key." The key Lummis is talking about is *choice*—the ability to choose our own self-talk.

Case Story of Larry

The amazing power which lies in our ability to choose is vividly demonstrated in the story of Larry, who underwent a life experience more shattering and painful than anything most people will ever have to endure. He survived that experience because, as Charles Fletcher Lummis put it, he chose to view misfortune and suffering as "outside his door."

Larry, a top-producing financial consultant, sat at a luncheon table after a seminar. The people at his table whom he had just met were painfully polite, going to near-ridiculous extremes to pretend they did not notice the scars on Larry's face and hands. Larry was familiar with other people's uneasiness, and he was a master in telling his story and encouraging people to feel relaxed.

"In case you're wondering about these scars," he said, "I don't mind talking about it. A few years ago, I survived a fiery plane crash."

"It must have been awful," someone ventured.

"Awful? Yes," Larry replied. "But when I got out of the plane, the first thing I thought was, 'I'm still alive!' They took me to the hospital, where I underwent the first surgery to reconstruct my face and arms. Altogether, I went through seventy-four operations—nine on my hands alone. What got me through it all was a choice I made. I decided to say to myself, 'This is just a temporary inconvenience.' Talking about that entire experience as a 'temporary inconvenience' made it bearable. Anything that has happened to me since then is microscopic in comparison."

Larry is an inspiring story and a memorable way to bring this section to a close. His courage shows so clearly the power of our choices.

SECTION WRAP-UP

To implant these truths in your mind and
fortify your power to recall, check the ideas
that are the most important to you:

❑ While I cannot control
every event in life, I
can control what I say
to myself about the
experience.

❑ I have the power to
choose how I define
any life experience.

❑ The way I define a life
experience is revealed
in how I talk to myself
about the experience.

❑ Some self-talk leads to
stress.

❑ Other self-talk leads to
motivation.

❑ What I say to myself
frequently has more
impact on my life than
the actual experience.

❑ The stress that
motivates is the stress
that I respond to by
taking action toward a
solution or toward
containment and
mastery.

❑ The most powerful way
to train myself to take
this action is with
systematic and
purposeful self-talk.

In the next section, you will learn what your parents, teachers and
employers may never have told you about stress and motivation.

SECTION

2

What They Didn't Tell You About Stress and Motivation

66 Many persons have a wrong idea of what constitutes true happiness. It is not attained through self-gratification but through fidelity to a worthy purpose. 99

—Helen Keller

SUCCESS SECRET

Knowledge is power

Since rapid change increases both
stress factors and the need for
motivation, it pays to keep up-to-date
on the dynamics of both.

THE ACCUMULATION OF STRESS

Harry, a big man with his collar open and tie loose, leaned forward with both hands chopping through the air to emphasize his excitement. ''Man-oh-man!'' he exclaimed. ''I wish I'd heard all this a few years ago. I didn't know what was happening to me! When I heard 'stress,' I thought it meant just being fed up. But I was going through honest-to-goodness stress and burnout and didn't even know it!''

Harry's face and eyes lit up, there was virtually a lightbulb shining over his head as he continued: ''There I was, eating all the time—not hungry, just grazing. I had trouble sleeping, trouble concentrating. I was getting so forgetful I thought I had Alzheimer's disease.

''I finally went to the doctor. The doc examined me and asked a lot of questions. I told her about my new job, about moving to a new city, and my putting on twenty pounds. Our daughter and her baby have moved back in with us for who knows how long. After the exam the doc assured me that my problems were stress-related. Now that I understand the whole stress thing better, it's obvious. But it wasn't then.''

Get a Medical Check-up

Take a lesson from Harry. If you are feeling a lot of stress, see your physician. There may be physiological causes of stress in addition to the psychological issues covered in this book. In addition, if you are interested in reading about the medical aspects of stress, see this comprehensive article in the *Journal of the American Medical Association:* ''The Concepts of Stress and Stress System Disorders.''

Knowledge About Stress and Motivation is Power

In this section we will delve into truths about stress that many people have never been told. Like Harry, you may see a light turn on as you connect these truths with your experience. Once you have an understanding of what stress is and how it affects you, you will have the power to manage it, direct it and use it as a motivating force.

After reading this section, you will be better equipped to:

- Spot early warning signals of trouble ahead

- Add more lift to your life with strong motivational ingredients

STRESS FACTORS

First, we will look at stress factors—the things that can drain and drag on us. The stresses that pull and tug can mount up, particularly in times of change. Most of us are not consciously aware of how much stress we are under or what we can do about it. But there are some simple, revealing insights and exercises to uncover those stress factors. The following insights and exercises will help you "turn on the light" and see how to handle stress even more effectively.

Insight #1:
You Can Predict When People
Are Most Likely to Feel Stressed

Pay special attention when:

- The person feels overwhelmed or flooded
- The stress is too intense
- The duration is too long
- The end is not in sight

In addition to the actual experience, consider how the feelings of stress skyrocket when a person says:

- I just can't cope.
- There is nothing I can do.
- This is too much.
- It will never end.
- I just can't handle it.

These statements handcuff a person's ability to think clearly and creatively when that ability is most needed. You can also predict stress when you discover these conditions:

- When a person feels he or she is alone
- When a person feels there is no one there for them
- When a person feels she or he is not appreciated

The reality here is feelings magnify stress. Some people may have an extensive support group within arms' reach, yet feel alone. Others may *feel* they are unappreciated, even when people appreciate them. On the other hand, people feel differently when they say to themselves:

- I find the right people at the right time.
- I take care of my own needs and wants, and I do it without hurting myself or others.
- I appreciate myself and what I do.

Insight #2:
You Can Approach Stress Two Ways

People may see stress as a wall and stop in their tracks. Or a person may see stress as a ladder—something to be recognized and ascended. The end result is standing at a higher place. Stress stimulates an organism. It challenges people to do more and be more than they would otherwise.

For a quick illustration of how important stress is, talk to someone who is in a convalescent hospital where there is little daily challenge. Without challenge, you can see the decrease in abilities in days. You may remember the studies of people in convalescent hospitals who were each given three or four potted plants to care for. People had to make decisions about how much to water, when to fertilize and where to capture the right sunlight. The decisions and challenges helped them keep more mental vitality.

Stress does stimulate us. We can either treat it as a wall or a ladder.

Insight #3:
Calling a "Time Out"
For a Few Minutes Helps Reduce Stress

Dr. Paul Ware recommends this quick time-out process. People who train themselves to use this surprisingly powerful tool can get themselves right back on track. A great way to learn the process is to say and use the following four techniques:

If I am feeling overwhelmed, I protect myself by taking time out for a few minutes so I can think clearly and creatively.

1. I relax and I breathe deeply.

2. I accept my feelings and the realities of my current situation.

3. I picture in my imagination how I want the situation to be.

4. I take some action to get there. I do something purposeful even if it is not the total solution. I work toward a solution or mastery of the situation.

A Baseball Memory Trick

An easy way to remember these four powerful techniques is to picture a baseball diamond with one technique at each base.

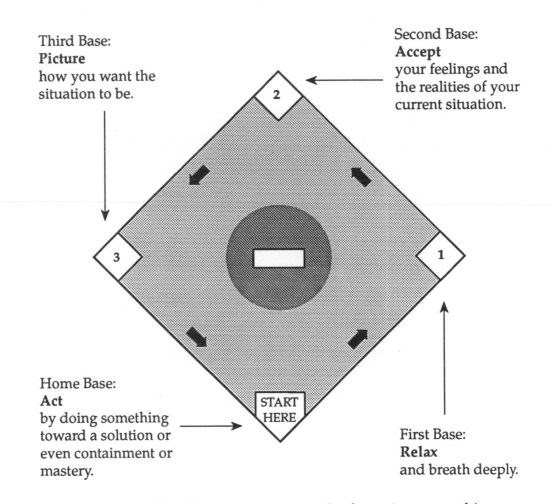

Third Base:
Picture
how you want the situation to be.

Second Base:
Accept
your feelings and the realities of your current situation.

Home Base:
Act
by doing something toward a solution or even containment or mastery.

First Base:
Relax
and breath deeply.

START HERE

People who feel considerable stress may spend a few minutes on this process three or four times a day. One man said he "stares intently at a printout on his desk and mentally works through the four bases. The results are so much better than telling myself, 'I can't cope. I'll never get caught up' and then feeling frozen for an hour."

Exercise:

Since this short time-out process has so much value for keeping stress in its place, take a moment now. Write the ideas on a card or in a handy place. Have them available for when you feel stress coming around the corner.

Insight #4:
You Can Spot Burnout by the
Three Specific Telltale Signals

Specific Signal A: Decreased Concentration

Here are two examples of someone having trouble concentrating.

Example One: A person who becomes very susceptible to interruptions. The interruptions can be from others as well as from herself.

Example Two: This person might be standing by a file drawer. He knows he walked over to get something, but once he put his hand on the drawer, he wonders, ''Now, what was I looking for?''

Specific Signal B: Feeling Suspicious of Other People's Joy

Imagine a person who is feeling burned out about life in general. If he sees someone who is whistling as he works and tackling tough jobs with gusto, the person who is experiencing burnout may narrow his eyes, scowl at the upbeat person, and mutter, ''That hypocrite! He can't really feel like that.''

Specific Signal C: Taking Things Personally

The person experiencing burnout often becomes self-focused. He questions events with, ''Why did this happen to *me*? Why did he say that to *me*?'' During burnout, empathy for others is on the back burner.

For example: A person walks down the office hallway. Approaching him from the other direction is a manager from another division—a nodding acquaintance and hardly a close friend. They pass in the hall, and the manager from the other division seems hurried, does not say ''Hello,'' and does not even make eye contact. Someone who is managing stress well would attach no particular importance to the incident. At most, the assumption would be that the other person is distracted or in a hurry. The burned-out person might begin to worry, ''Why is the manager mad at me?''

Exercise:

Do you identify with any of the burnout signals? If so, which ones?

_____

_____

Insight #5:
You Can Predict Stressful Burnout
by Spotting the Eight General Signals

The terms stress and burnout are often used interchangeably. The list below features the eight general signals of burnout. See if you find yourself or people in your life described in this list.

The Eight General Signals of Burnout

1. Communicating Less

A person with this signal might say less at meetings. He might feel dismayed whenever the phone rings. Rather than talking with his family at breakfast, he reads the cereal box.

2. Feeling Less Energy

This shows up in different ways. The most common description is feeling as though a person's gears are turning; however, there is sawdust slowing down the gears.

3. Experiencing Lower Productivity

The person with lower productivity usually notices it long before any one else. He might go home at night and ask himself ''What did I accomplish today?'' He is hard-pressed for a good answer.

4. Late More Often for Work or Appointments

It's a logical flow to see how less energy leads to being late more often.

5. Sleep Disturbance

Sleep disturbance takes different forms. The person may have trouble going to sleep and then wake up in the middle of the night—usually around 3 A.M. After that, he may not be able to go *back* to sleep. Sleep disturbance can take another form; the person may want to sleep all the time. If someone is having this type of sleep disturbance, he might turn on the television and drift into sleep long before the end of a program.

THE EIGHT GENERAL SIGNALS OF BURNOUT (continued)

6. Appetite Disturbance

This condition can go two ways. Unplanned weight loss is the most common signal. Or it can exhibit itself as unplanned weight gain. The person with appetite disturbance may want to eat all the time. Tip-offs include after-dinner grazing, looking into the refrigerator, and rummaging through the cupboards. The tip-off is that the person is eating when there is no physical hunger.

7. Preoccupied with Health and Body

It is good to be conscientious about exercise and good eating. But people experiencing stress and burnout often become highly focused on their physical selves. They think and talk about their bodily functions and sensations much of the time.

8. Decreased Wants

This is another important signal. The person loses interest in the world. Here is a quick experiment.

> Picture an interviewer handing two people each a yellow-lined pad with this request: "Write down everything you want to do, re-do, read, write, reorganize, discuss, see, hear, visit, clean out, catch up, or buy."

- The person who has little stress or who is managing stress well will take the pad and the pen will fly. He or she will fill up four or five pages without a let-up and still have plenty of ideas.

- The person who feels stressed and burned out is another picture. He or she will stare at the pad, write a few lines, sigh and put down the pen.

Insight #6:
Burnout Is Stressful and Common, but It Is Not Mandatory

Do not feel cheated if you are not feeling burned out. Even though someone says, "Everybody in this job gets burned out," do not believe it.

Insight #7:
Language Can Alert You to Stress

A recent informal study conducted in a major American corporation showed convincingly that language is an important indicator of stress. The study was conducted over a seven-year period and involved interviews with over 4,000 people in everyday work situations. Researchers studied verbatim transcripts of these interviews.

People who described themselves as under stress tended to use certain kinds of statements over three times more frequently than other individuals. The results were consistent. A clear link between stress and stressful language was established.

Ten of the most common stressful statements were listed in Section 1, and they are repeated below. Read through those statements and place a check before any that you recall saying a number of times in the last week.

☐ My situation is different. ☐ I tried it once, and it didn't work.

☐ There's nothing I can do. ☐ It's not that easy.

☐ It will never work. ☐ You don't know the people I work with.

☐ I don't have time. ☐ It doesn't feel natural.

☐ There's too much to do. ☐ I know this already.

Exercise:

When you think about yourself and these statements, how would you rate yourself on a scale of 1 to 10? (1 = Feeling a lot of stress. The road is bumpy. 10 = Feeling no stress. It's a smooth, clear road ahead.)

What changes might you make after looking at the list of stressful language? This list shows the intimate link between stress and the language of our self-talk. Think about how much impact language has on our beliefs and behavior—especially when we repeat our messages to ourselves again and again.

**Insight #8:
Exercise Is the Most Important
Way to Reduce Stressful Burnout**

Getting a good supply of oxygen to your brain still tops the list of ways to reduce stress. Here is the reason: Oxygen helps you think clearly and creatively. Yet exercise is the last thing most people feel like doing when they feel stress.

The good news is that to make a difference, you do not need to run a marathon. The exercise that gets the most points in terms of the best benefit with the least risk is walking. Walking only two miles a day is so important that many therapists recommend it as a prerequisite for starting treatment for severe states of burnout. Whether it is walking or another form of exercise, carve out time for yourself.

Taking care of yourself in positive ways like exercise helps you be your best for all the people in your life.

**Insight #9:
Take Care of Your Own Needs and Wants
in Positive Ways**

It is obvious. When you satisfy your own needs and wants in constructive ways, you have more energy to take action. You avoid the temptation that often combines with stress: feeling like other people should be doing more for you. You have an easier time tackling the responsibilities you face. When you keep your psychological tank on "full," everyone benefits. You are a much better person to be around. You can serve others much more effectively.

Keeping Your Tank Full

In terms of how well you are keeping yourself filled with psychological satisfaction, where would your gauge be right now?

As one woman laughingly related, "I used to think the line was 'Love your neighbor *instead* of yourself.' The real message is 'Love your neighbor *as* yourself.'" Take care of yourself. Do it in ways that do not hurt yourself, others, or your situation.

MOTIVATION—A STRONG SENSE OF DIRECTION CUTS THE STRESS

You rarely read in the popular press about the importance of purpose and direction in reducing stress. Yet, a sense of purpose and direction in our lives—a sense of motivation—is truly the key to managing and conquering stress. Now we will look at the positive side of the picture—motivation.

The word motivation comes from the Latin movere, which means ''to move.'' Motivation suggests energy, drive, persistence, accomplishments, teamwork, satisfaction. These are things we all want, things every organization wants. Yet, we often overlook the core meaning of motivation.

Motivation Means Motive

Motivation means having a strong inner incentive to action—*action* toward a goal, *action* with a purpose. Consequently, being motivated means knowing where you want to go. It means knowing your dreams, objectives and chosen destination.

The section which follows will help you gain a stronger sense of your own motives and motivation factors.

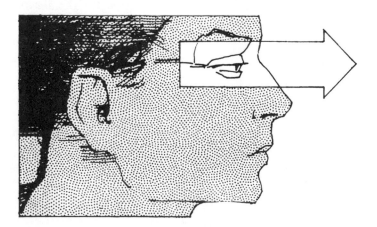

THE MAN-ON-THE-STREET INTERVIEW

For each of the following exercises, rate yourself on a scale of one to five.

1. **Your Lifetime Objectives**—Imagine a man-on-the-street interviewer for a television show shoving a microphone in front of you. "You will win one million dollars," he says, "if you have written down your lifetime objectives. Ah-ah-ah! No fair writing them on the spot!" How much will you win? Rate yourself on a scale of 1 to 10.

   1 ——————————————————————— 10
   1 = Not one cent.   10 = A $1 million jackpot.

2. **Your Organizational Mission and Vision**—The same man-on-the-street interviewer offers you another million if you can accurately explain your organization's mission and objectives. Saying, "But nobody ever told me!" does not count. Can you explain it or not? That is all the interviewer wants to know. How much will you win?

   1 ——————————————————————— 10
   1 = Zilch.   10 = The full $1 million.

3. **Your Three-Year Objectives**—How clear and specific are the goals and mental word pictures for what you want to accomplish during the next three years?

   1 ——————————————————————— 10
   1 = I have been meaning to get around to that.   10 = Clear and specific.

4. **Your One-Year Targets for Each Priority Area**—Do you have clear, written goals for where you want to be one year from now in each important area of your life?

   1 ——————————————————————— 10
   1 = Could we change the subject?   10 = I have them all written out.

5. **Your Dream**—Do you have a dream that is so important to you that whenever you have a spare moment, your thoughts automatically turn to ways to accomplish that dream? (Your dream may already be in your lifetime objectives or your organizational mission.)

   1 ——————————————————————— 10
   1 = I'm just trying to survive the day.   10 = My dream pulls me through life.

6. **Your Passion**—Do you support a cause that is bigger than yourself, your family, or your friends? Is it a cause to which you devote time and energy each week?

   1 ——————————————————————— 10
   1 = I wish I did.   10 = Oh, yes! The most wonderful cause in the world!

Stress That Motivates

THE POWER OF PURPOSE

Reflect on your answers. Were your winnings and your ratings as high as you want them? If your answer is:

YES:

Congratulate yourself. You are among a select group of achievers. You have a head start on getting everything you want in life. Plus, you have a head start on being a valued person in the lives of your family, friends, employers, employees and customers.

NO:

Are you embarrassed by some of your answers to these questions? Worry not. You don't have to reveal them to anyone else. This exercise is for your benefit. It helps you get a better picture of your life—your stress level and your motivation level. You are now in that select minority of people who have a better understanding of their own motivation level. That understanding is a big doorway to taking purposeful action for improvement.

Now, go back through the questions. Imagine yourself scoring at the high end of each scale! Picture how good it feels to have a clear direction and purpose in life. Then commit yourself to taking whatever action is needed to build your passionate sense of direction and motivation.

For Extra Credit

The lights over a stadium at night are no brighter than the lights you have in your life by having up-to-date answers to the questions. Most people need time to think through the answers to the man-on-the-street interview.

When is a likely day and time for you to carve out some good thinking time?

_____

_____

What is a timetable for completion that will motivate you?

_____

_____

It is never too late to do this thinking as you will see in the next case story.

STRESS AND THE MOTIVATIONAL POWER OF A DREAM— CELEBRATING POP'S 80th

''A dream did it.'' Carol, a tall, energetic executive in her early 40s, smiled musingly at the group around the table as she shared a story from her family experience. ''A dream helped my 79-year-old father-in-law survive tremendous stress,'' she said. ''I believe it was his dream that pulled him through to his eightieth birthday.

''The doctors told us Pops was living on oxygen and borrowed time and that he had only a few more weeks to live. I remembered how he always enjoyed having a dream or big goal to work toward. So that evening I sat down beside his bed in our upstairs bedroom and I threw him a challenge: 'Pops, how about hosting a birthday party for yourself a year from now? Invite the five kids and their families. You know, Pops, you can't take it with you. Why don't you pay for the party and the travel for everyone too?'

''Even though he was weak and on oxygen most of the time, Pops spent the entire year planning the food, checking which grandchild wanted to share a room with whom, fine-tuning the schedule, organizing awards for the basketball contest, and tracking down the best air fares. I saw him literally pulled through that last year by his dream.

''To the doctors' amazement, Pops made it to his 80th birthday party. That dream gave us all the pleasure of an extra year of his life.''

A strong motivational draw helps us punch through times of stress. Whether we are in our twenties, forties, sixties or eighties, a powerful sense of direction and purpose can add to our enjoyment, our productivity and our lifespan.

SECTION WRAP-UP

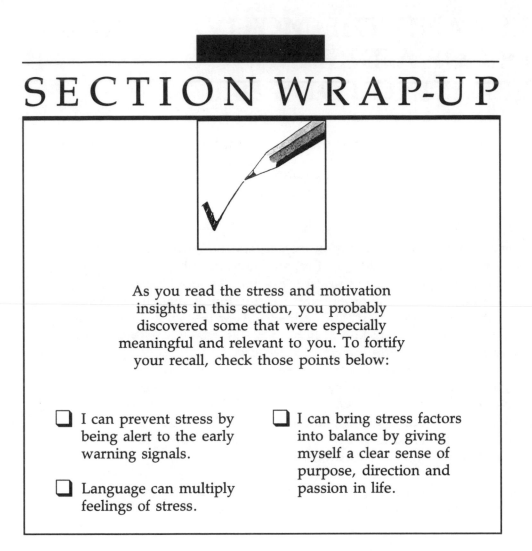

As you read the stress and motivation insights in this section, you probably discovered some that were especially meaningful and relevant to you. To fortify your recall, check those points below:

❑ I can prevent stress by being alert to the early warning signals.

❑ Language can multiply feelings of stress.

❑ I can bring stress factors into balance by giving myself a clear sense of purpose, direction and passion in life.

In the next section you will discover a shortcut for getting a new and powerful perspective on stress factors.

SECTION

3

Your Stress-Motivation Profile

**The Serenity Prayer
of Reinhold Niebuhr**

❛❛God grant me the serenity to accept

the things I cannot change, the courage

to change the things I can, and the wisdom

to know the difference.❜❜

SUCCESS SECRET

Charting your stress and
motivation factors makes it easier
to take purposeful action.

WHY A STRESS-MOTIVATION PROFILE?

Lori took a deep breath, leaned back in her chair, and let her hands drop toward the floor. As she looked at the others in the seminar room, her body language reflected her new calmness.

''Seeing my Stress-Motivation Profile was a relief,'' she told the group. ''Once I charted my profile, I could see things in black and white. Now I know why I was feeling so stressed, and now I see there are some things I can do.''

Lori looked the part of a successful woman. No one would have suspected that when she walked into the seminar two hours earlier, she felt as if her life was crumbling. Yet, that is exactly what her Stress-Motivation Profile showed. In this section, we will look at Lori's profile as well as two others. At the end of this section, you will have a chance to put together your own Stress-Motivation Profile. Here is Lori's profile.

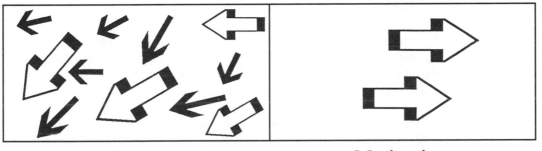

| **Stress** | **Motivation** |

Notice the arrows in the Stress box. They look like someone set off a bomb in an arrow factory. Each arrow represents a specific stress factor in Lori's life. Clearly, she was under a lot of stress. While some of the other participants in the seminar chose not to explain the stress arrows in their profiles, Lori shared with the group some of the specifics behind her stress arrows:

- She had been deserted by her husband less than a year before.
- She had recently been transferred to a strange city, where she was seeking to establish herself as a sales producer in a tough region.
- She was having a hard time finding good housing in her price range.
- She was having trouble finding child care for her two-year-old.
- Recently, she had been sick and her income dropped.

''No wonder I've been so stressed out!'' Lori related. ''Doing the profile was the first time I had ever taken inventory of the stress in my life. Some of these are things I can change, some I can't. Now I know where to start.''

WHY A STRESS-MOTIVATION PROFILE? (continued)

Looking at the Motivation side of her Profile, Lori saw that she had two very strong motivating factors: Her two-year-old daughter and her job. These factors kept her moving forward despite her stressful circumstances.

As a result of doing her Stress-Motivation Profile, Lori decided that there were several actions she could take to better manage the stress factors in her life:

- Cut back on expenses in order to afford a live-in nanny
- Set and achieve key account goals in her new job
- Join a church and a single parent support group
- Meet new friends

A Path to Action

Perhaps you identify with how Lori felt before she did her Stress-Motivation Profile. Perhaps you know you are under a lot of stress but you have not stopped to analyze why or where that stress is coming from. You are ready for a change. You want relief.

Well, relief is on the way. This is a chapter that will help you understand your stress and motivation factors and what kind of action you can take. You will also gain a welcome sense of calm by putting your profile together.

As you interact with this chapter and work through the exercises, you will gain the understanding and tools to:

- Discover a new perspective on your situation
- Reduce your stress level
- Feel more energized and effective
- Accomplish the right things

Keep these ideas in mind as you study two more interesting case stories that show very different situations.

MEL—FEW STRESS FACTORS AND NO MOTIVATION FACTORS

Mel, a balding man in his mid-fifties, tugged at the V-neck of his brown sweater as he shared with the others in the class. "It was hard for me to admit that I even needed to attend an out-placement seminar," he said. "When I first got laid off, I thought it was the best thing that ever happened to me. I had hated that job. I had always felt like I was under someone's thumb. I had put in long hours every day, plus a forty-five minute bus commute each way. I did that five days a week for thirty-two lousy years. Then the company was sold, and I got a layoff package: one week's pay for every year, plus four weeks' vacation. That's thirty-six weeks full pay for doing nothing! That was going to be heaven—or so I thought.

"I used to dream of having weeks on end with nothing to do, no responsibilities. I had a lot of stress in my job. For a few years there, I even had a fair amount of stress at home, as well as taking care of mother after her stroke. She passed away three years ago.

"Here I am, living the life of Riley, with no responsibilities, no stress. I even watch game shows on TV during the day. Order a pizza whenever I feel like it. Sleep as late as I want—ten, eleven, even noon sometimes. Some days I never leave the house. I kid you not, this is what my Stress-Motivation Profile looks like." Mel produced his Profile and showed it to the rest of the seminar participants. Yes, it looked like this, completely blank.

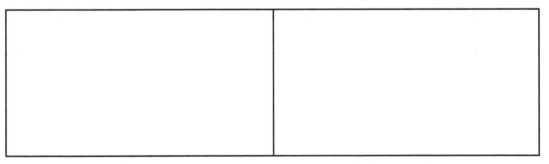

| Stress | Motivation |

Mel continued, "A few weeks ago, it hit me. I didn't have any stress in my life, but I didn't have much to live for, either. I mean, eating, sleeping, and watching TV—what kind of life is that? So now I'm looking for work again. But this time, I want to go back to work better prepared to manage stress. I've decided some stress is good for me. I can work and still have the weekends to look forward to."

The next profile shows such a different picture.

ANNE—HER ARROWS FLY IN FORMATION

"I tell you, I could have ripped those little monsters apart!" Anne confessed. "Last month, these two twelve-year-old boys stopped my eight-year-old daughter on the school yard and pulled her jeans down! Now she's scared to go back to school!

"I take her to counseling two nights a week. It's slow, but it's helping. My daughter is tough, and I know she will get over it. I'm working with some other parents and we're getting better supervision on the play yard.

"Change takes so much time. It's the same thing at work. We're finally getting more women into jobs with some decent pay. I have a meeting on Wednesday to get the word out. But everything is work—hard work. I've been in this job for five years, and I'm still working to get my crew leader assignment made permanent.

"But when it comes through, I'll be making more money. I just keep at it, and I keep telling myself, 'One day at a time.'"

When Anne showed the group her Stress-Motivation Profile, it looked like this:

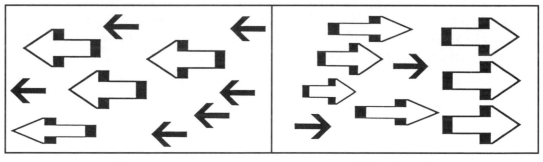

Stress   **Motivation**

Anne filled both sides of her profile with arrows—large, medium, and small ones. She sees herself as having to deal with a lot of stress. She also sees herself as being highly motivated.

The significant feature of Anne's profile is that all of the arrows are parallel. All the arrows fly in formation. She has a lot of stress, and she has learned to contain and master her stress by taking action toward solutions. Although her stress factors are numerous, she is mastering them. She also has a high level of motivation, and her motivation factors are all directed along a single trajectory, aimed toward a common goal: a better life for herself, her three children and work associates—particularly women workers.

WHAT THE PROFILES SHOW

The three Profiles illustrate a wide range of situations and reactions:

► Lori had too few motivation factors. Her box full of stress factors exploded chaotically. Her Profile is giving her the understanding to make meaningful changes in her life.

► Mel had no motivation factors and no stress factors. Although he dreamed about no stress, it did not deliver satisfaction.

► Anne's Profile is the picture of emotional health, even though she is in a crucible of stress. Her stress and motivation factors are controlled and aligned. She is managing her stress—and her life.

You, too, can gain even more control over your life. The Stress-Motivation Profile will help you decide on the best action for you to take.

Your Stress-Motivation Profile

Charting your own Stress-Motivation Profile is quick and easy. There is no better time to do it than right now. Begin by describing your own situation—including the life experiences about which you feel stress and also the dreams, goals, passions and interests about which you feel motivated. Jot down a few key words for each major area in your life. Mark which are stressors and which are motivators.

_____

_____

_____

_____

_____

_____

_____

Before you put together the graphic representation of your situation, reflect on the ideas you have crystalized by doing previous exercises.

YOUR STRESS-MOTIVATION PROFILE

These suggestions will save you time as you draw your Stress-Motivation Profile:

Represent large factors with large arrows, small factors with small arrows. If your stress factors are contained and mastered, represent them as arrows moving to the left in parallel formation. If the stressors are exploding out of control, show the arrows in chaotic and haphazard directions.

To chart your own Stress-Motivation Profile, you can use the two boxes below.

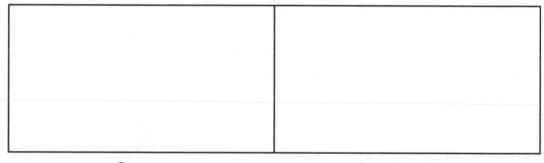

| **Stress** | **Motivation** |

Drawing a Stress-Motivation Profile helps you see what is happening to you and what needs to be done. Stress becomes easier to handle when you:

- Have a compensating balance of motivational factors to keep you moving toward your goals, and

- Have your stress factors contained and mastered so that they don't pull you apart.

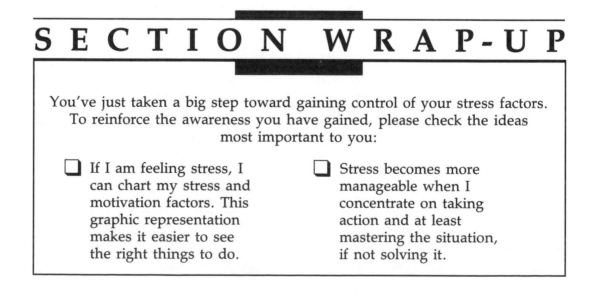

SECTION WRAP-UP

You've just taken a big step toward gaining control of your stress factors. To reinforce the awareness you have gained, please check the ideas most important to you:

❑ If I am feeling stress, I can chart my stress and motivation factors. This graphic representation makes it easier to see the right things to do.

❑ Stress becomes more manageable when I concentrate on taking action and at least mastering the situation, if not solving it.

SECTION

4

Purposeful Self-Talk:
A Great Place to Start

❝ Sow a thought,
    and you reap an act;
Sow an act,
    and you reap a habit;
Sow a habit,
    and you reap a character;
Sow a character,
    and you reap a destiny. ❞

—Samuel Smiles

SUCCESS SECRET

When you want a change, there is an easy and effective way to start.

Change what you say to yourself.

THE POWER OF PURPOSEFUL SELF-TALK

In the next few pages, you will discover new dimensions in the power of what you say to yourself. You will explore:

► What happens when you instill purpose in what you say to yourself

► Ways to use purposeful self-talk to:
  • Save time
  • Feel better
  • Get the right things done

► How repetition wins

► The relationship between self-talk and feelings

Firestorm or Fireplace

By now, it is very clear: What we say to ourselves about our situation will either stress or motivate us. How tragic that so few people really understand this fundamental dynamic!

Left unattended, self-talk can turn into a raging firestorm of negativity. When a wildfire races out of control, flames leap from tree to tree, housetop to housetop. Houses explode in flames and are destroyed in seconds.

Negative, unattended self-talk can be just as devastating in a person's life as that firestorm. It destroys creativity. It damages confidence. It degrades productivity. It becomes a self-fulfilling prophecy of doom and gloom, an ever-worsening feedback loop of discouragement.

However, when self-talk is directed, contained and purposeful, it provides light and warmth—just like the cozy, soothing blaze in a fireplace. Hold that picture in your mind for a moment. Think of yourself sitting in front of a fireplace on a rainy evening. Breathe in the resinous pungency of the burning logs. Feel the warmth of the glowing coals. Consider how protected and safe you feel next to that dancing fire while the cold wind rattles the tree branches outside.

Fireplace or firestorm: it is the same power. But what a difference. In the fireplace, that power is contained. It has a place. It has a purpose. It is controlled.

Self-talk is a power like fire. Uncontrolled, it can destroy. Take charge of it, direct it, give it purpose, and it can profoundly change your life for the better.

PROOF POSITIVE: AN EXPERIMENT WITH TWO LISTS

The following experiment shows how words shape your feelings and influence your behavior. Each of the two lists below takes just a minute or two to read. As you read them you may be surprised at the impact they make on your thinking and feeling.

Stress List: Downers and Drainers

As you read this collection of stressful and unproductive self-talk statements, be aware of your feelings. You will get the most from this experiment if you read the sentences out loud.

I can't stand it.

I just can't deal with it anymore.

I feel terrible.

I just don't know what to do.

I'm always so far behind.

That is so stupid.

I shouldn't have to do this.

I'm just waiting for someone to notice.

There is too much to do.

Nobody appreciates me.

Everyone is so uncooperative.

There's nothing I can do.

Experiment:

On a scale of one to ten, rate yourself on the following questions.

1. How do you feel right now?

1 ——————————————————————— **10**

1 = Drained, discouraged.　　　　　10 = Great! Top of the world.

2. How energized are you to take constructive action?

1 ——————————————————————— **10**

1 = Tired. Blah. I need a nap.　　　　10 = I'm going to move mountains.

3. After reading the downers and drainers list, what is the probability that you will make continuous improvements in your life?

1 ——————————————————————— **10**

1 = I pass.　　　　　　　　　　10 = You can count on me.

Motivation List: Lifters and Leaders

Now read the second list—aloud, if possible—and be aware of your thinking and feeling responses as you read.

I always have choices.

There is always something I can do.

I turn problems into opportunities.

I keep myself in a good mood.

I picture what I want in wonderful detail.

I "grab fifteen." It is incredible how much I can accomplish in fifteen minutes.

I finish fully and I feel good.

I forgive and I feel free.

This is a good day.

I help people get what they want.

I ask for what I want.

I take good care of myself.

I solve problems without blaming myself or others.

I prevent problems.

I give myself a great start because I wrap up the tough top priority first.

I do it now.

Exercise:

Now, take your "mental pulse." Tune in to your feelings and your thoughts. On a scale of one to ten, rate yourself on the following questions:

1. How do you feel right now?

1 ———————————————————— **10**

1 = Drained. Discouraged.   10 = Great! Top of the world.

2. How energized are you to take constructive action?

1 ———————————————————— **10**

1 = Tired. Blah. Need a nap.   10 = I am going to move mountains.

3. What is the probability that you will make continuous improvements in your life?

1 ———————————————————— **10**

1 = I pass.   10 = You can count on me.

There is no question which list leaves you feeling best, feeling productive, feeling energized to take on the world.

THREE IMPORTANT QUESTIONS

Question #1: What Makes Self-Talk Work?

The secret is *purposeful action.* Rather than letting random ideas float around in every direction, *shape your self-talk around the purposes you select.* That is what makes them motivational. Make sure everything you say to yourself contributes to where you want to go. Also, make sure that your self-talk encourages you to take *action.*

Two Kinds of Purposeful Self-Talk (Reinforcements)

Purposeful self-talk—There are two essential kinds of purposeful self-talk:

1. Word pictures that describe the objectives and destinations you want to reach.

2. Processes are those repetitive steps that help you reach your desired destinations.

A quick example will show how these two forms of purposeful self-talk work. Barbara used a word picture to imagine herself at her goal weight, wearing a size seven red dress. She also used the process of telling herself ''When I feel tempted to graze, I reach for some carrot sticks.'' The combination of these two forms of purposeful self-talk enabled her to reach her objective. You will tap into the power of word pictures more fully in Section 7.

Question #2: Don't You Have to Do More Than Just Say Things to Yourself?

The answer is a loud and clear, ''yes.'' Self-talk is merely the beginning. Improving what you say to yourself is not the end: *more productive action is.*

Think of it this way: self-talk that does not produce productive action is like buying a boat and leaving it tied up at the dock. Productive behavior is the ultimate goal of purposeful self-talk, just as an enjoyable sail on the lake is the ultimate goal of buying a boat.

Purposeful Thinking Prompts Purposeful Behavior

Purposeful self-talk is a process for training yourself to do the right thing at the right time. Plant constructive ideas in your mind over and over. Nurture them, and they will grow. The ideas become habits. Then, when the opportunity comes, you automatically say the right thing to yourself. This in turn encourages you to *do* the right thing.

The case story on the next page shows how one person changed her behavior by first changing her thinking.

CASE STORY: *The Scavenger Hunt*

Rachael sat back in her conference room chair, a woman in her mid-thirties, black turtleneck and designer jeans, no-nonsense short hair, and big gold earrings. She described herself as a street-savvy woman who had worked herself up through the ranks to a responsible job. However, she confessed that she struggled with clutter every day. "I waste so much time looking for things," she said self-reproachfully. "You wouldn't believe the stacks of paper on my desk. And the stacks on the table. And my file drawers are a disaster."

Every day, big chunks of Rachael's time were chewed up by "scavenger hunts." She may have misplaced a letter, a file folder, some receipts, her keys, her earrings—it was always something. She fumed about the wasted time but, until now, did not know how to solve the problem.

"Two months ago, I misplaced some travel receipts. After almost two hours of fruitless searching, I threw up my hands and said, 'Enough is enough!' I suddenly realized that I actually knew the answer," she concluded, "I was just not doing the things that I knew would help me. When I was a kid, my mother always told me, 'A place for everything and everything in its place.' Every time she told me that, I used to grind my molars!

"I started repeating to myself an idea I had heard in a seminar: 'No temporary parking places. In place or in use.' I wrote that idea on a three-by-five card and kept it by my computer. I repeated the idea to myself morning, noon and night. I even pictured myself with a fistful of twenty-dollar bills from turning in my receipts and expenses.

"It's funny. After picturing the cash in hand and reading that sign to myself for only a month, I started to change what I did. I would almost be ready to toss a folder on a pile on my desk or stuff a receipt in my coat pocket—and then I would smile and encourage myself 'No temporary parking places. In place or in use!' Then I would walk to the filing cabinet and slip that folder into its regular parking place. Or I would put that receipt in the right pocket in my wallet.

"Clutter has always been such a hassle for me. Now it's almost fun finding ways to keep myself organized. Now, I am spending less and less time on 'scavenger hunts'!"

The key: Purposeful thinking really *does* prompt purposeful behavior!

Question #3: But Aren't You Telling Yourself Something That Isn't True?

''You are saying it on faith,'' Elizabeth shared. A statuesque woman, her gray hair gracefully swept up and held by a tailored bow, Elizabeth radiated assurance as she spoke to the others around the table. ''The book of *Hebrews* defines it this way: 'Faith is being sure of what we hope for and certain of what we do not see.' When you plant your hope of future results in the present, you exercise your faith. It is like picturing a full-grown oak tree when you plant an acorn in the ground.''

You add the energizing element of faith when you actively state and affirm a hope as if it has already happened. And repetition compels faith.

Repetition Wins

Advertising companies have understood the power of *repetition* for decades. Winning the race for the position in people's minds depends on repetition. No one deliberately decides to learn the messages that advertisers broadcast our way; yet, chances are each of us knows how to finish a popular slogan or jingle.

Repetition invariably makes a profound impact—whether for good or harm. Brian was a seven-year-old boy—blonde, exuberant and lovable. One evening, as his mother was helping him with his addition, Brian shoved his books across the kitchen table and grumped, ''Just forget it, Mom! I'm stupid. I can't do math.''

Even though the standardized tests he had taken at school showed a strong aptitude for math, Brian scores D's in his arithmetic class. Even though he is a bright child, his self-talk is tearing him down. He repeats to himself, ''I'm stupid. I can't do math.'' Worst of all, he is putting his belief into action.

Repetition does win—and tragically so, in Brian's case.

We Become What We Think About

We *do* become what we think about. This is hardly a new idea—although it is a much-neglected one. Purposeful self-talk reinforces the best in us so that we can *do* our best and *be* our best.

SECTION WRAP-UP

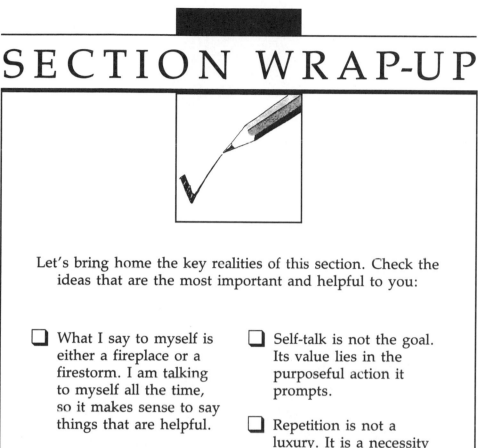

Let's bring home the key realities of this section. Check the ideas that are the most important and helpful to you:

☐ What I say to myself is either a fireplace or a firestorm. I am talking to myself all the time, so it makes sense to say things that are helpful.

☐ Some statements drain energy and trigger stress.

☐ Other statements lift, direct and motivate.

☐ When I put purpose into my self-talk, I triple the benefits.

☐ Self-talk is not the goal. Its value lies in the purposeful action it prompts.

☐ Repetition is not a luxury. It is a necessity for winning. I can train myself for success by repeating positive, purposeful reinforcements.

☐ Starting an improvement with self-talk makes sense because it is effective, totally within my control, and it takes only minutes a day.

In the next section, you will see how to become your own best coach through purposeful self-talk.

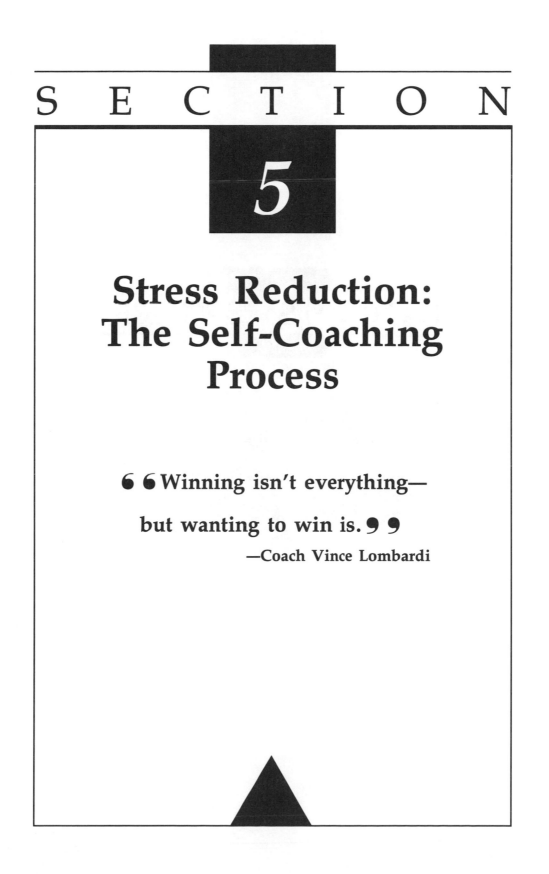

SECTION

5

Stress Reduction:
The Self-Coaching
Process

❝Winning isn't everything—

but wanting to win is.❞

—Coach Vince Lombardi

SUCCESS SECRET

Be your own coach.
Whether you are ahead or behind,
keep on coaching yourself.

"WHAT IF OTHER PEOPLE ARE CAUSING YOUR STRESS?"

This question pops up first in seminars on stress. And it is easy to see why this is such a common concern. In a stressful situation, it is natural for us to respond, "This person needs to change, this situation needs to change. If only the circumstances were different, I wouldn't have this stress." In times of stress it is much harder for us to say, "I need to change."

It is a paradox. If we follow our instincts and try to change other people, our stress will actually *increase*. But when we make a decision to *change ourselves* and take action toward a solution, we become stronger and the stress loses its power over us. There is often a fringe benefit. Once a person stops pressuring others and starts solving his part of the problem, the other people often change.

To change ourselves in times of stress, we need to become our own coaches. We need to learn to talk to ourselves so that we can turn our external stress factors into internal motivation for change and improvement.

In this section, you will be hearing about the self-coaching process. Most of the principles you will gain in this section come from the example of Doug. Through his story, you will polish your skills in these areas:

- What to do when confronted by difficult people

- How to fix your part of the problem without owning the other person's part

- How to use self-coaching techniques to tackle stress

As you read and do the exercises, remember: good coaches do not give up just because the team is down a few points. Good coaches are there for the wins and the losses. Never give up on yourself! Keep on coaching yourself whether you are winning or losing. Use the powerful techniques of self-coaching and enjoy the benefits of reduced stress, increased power, stronger relationships and more effective motivation.

EXERCISE AHEAD

WARM-UP EXERCISE:

To get the most from the case story in this section, first spend a few moments concentrating on *your* story.

1. Describe a particularly stressful time in your life:

_____

2. What did you do in that situation to turn it around? In reflecting on that turnaround, what did you do to help yourself recover from that stressful experience?

_____

3. What lessons did you learn from that situation?

_____

Now, read Doug's story. In his own words, he shares his time of stress, his turnaround experience and his personal paradigm shift—the enhancement in his thinking that enabled him to pull out of his stressful nose-dive.

DOUG'S STORY:

Stress and All Those Turkeys

''I never said I had a stress problem. I said I had a turkey problem,'' Doug announced. He settled his 6'2" frame, lean from ten years of racketball twice a week, into the conference-room chair. Turning on his ready smile, Doug sighed, loosened his tie and tossed his jacket across the table.

''Turkeys in traffic,'' he grumbled. ''Turkeys in management. Too many turkeys. Everyone taking a piece out of me. I just want the people around me to stop acting like a big bunch of inconsiderate turkeys.''

In bits and pieces Doug revealed his story. A sales representative for an electronics company, he was struggling with professional burnout, complicated by a 20-year marriage gone stale and the pressures of raising two teenage boys. Anger and futility had trapped him in a vise-grip of stressful resentment day after day.

''People at work are so out to lunch. Getting ahead around here—its all politics. They made me a sales manager two years ago. After a month, I told them to keep it. Transfer me back to being a sales rep.''

More Motivated

Doug clenched and unclenched his teeth as he continued. "Last week my boss sat down with me and gave me *another* talk about how I need to be more motivated. I thought to myself, 'Yeah, I sure do need more motivation and just exactly when was he going to motivate me? What a jerk!' Turkeys all day long, and then I get it from my boss and then from my wife when I get home. It isn't fair.

"Sometimes I think the only appreciation I get is from my golden retriever, Goldie. As soon as I walk in the door, I head for that dog and we have us a good wrestling match. My wife Brenda has a fit. Says our rough play sends a cloud of dog hairs floating over the couches and chairs. She says I should take the dog outside. I can hear her now. Nag, nag, nag. She complains to our sons, 'I don't know how long your dad expects me to put up with his antics. Here he is. Rushes into the house, makes a mess, wolfs down his food, and takes off. Dirty dishes and dog hairs. That's how you know he's been here!'"

Doug chuckled mirthlessly. "Funny, huh? All I get from my wife is static. Nothing is good enough for her. She's always trying to change me. What does she want—perfection? No wonder I'm outta there every chance I get to coach my son's basketball team. We're in last place, but we are going to turn things around. I keep on telling those kids 'You can do it.' Then I see something sink in and they get out there and do it. When a kid calls me "Heeeey Coach," that's the best! Brenda nags me about the time I spend on basketball, but coaching the kids is the only place I'm a hero."

Pressures Plus

"Between my boss and my wife, I've had it.

"I know my job's on the line. Sales are down. But everyone is having quota problems. What do you expect with all these rumors about consolidations and cutbacks? Sure, I'm getting a few complaint calls. I don't have time to follow up on every little detail. With all the meetings and paperwork, how does the company expect me to sell anything? Sure, I tell myself to stop procrastinating on the paperwork, but I feel buried sometimes. I have to put up with piles of garbage.

"Day after day I'm out there by myself dealing with inconsiderate turkeys. I don't dare talk back to customers. And I can't say anything to my boss. I just have to keep on eating it. Yesterday I got so ticked off, I felt like my head was going to explode."

Doug slumped down in his chair. "But it's not just my head I'm afraid of losing. If things don't change, I may lose my job . . . and my wife. Everything."

DOUG'S STORY (continued)

The Turning Point

"Remember the other day when I said things had to change? Well, it's beginning to sink in that maybe I'm the one who needs to change." Doug sat down and tossed his coat aside as he had before. This time, however, he looked more relaxed. The stress lines in his forehead were less furrowed.

"Right after that, the doctor told me I had to work on getting over feeling so down. He said I was already doing the most important thing—exercising. But he got out his little white note pad and prescribed three things:

- Be more forgiving and less irritated.

- Ask for what you want rather than not saying anything and resenting everything.

- Talk about your feelings rather than slamming doors.

"You can imagine how I hate that 'get in the hot tub and talk about your feelings' stuff. The doc did say that I will be able to control my feelings better when I put them into words. I don't know about that. But I know I have to do something. Maybe I should try that seminar on stress and self-talk that my boss has been trying to shove down my throat. I know I need something."

Coaching Yourself

"Soon after that, I sat cooling my heels in a customer's reception area. I picked up a golf magazine. As I was thumbing through it, an article about my favorite pro caught my eye. He described how he said things to himself to keep his concentration each game. The idea looked different. More sports related. Well, I ripped out the article and stuck it in my coat pocket.

"A week later I stopped at a coffee shop about 11 o'clock in the morning to get organized. I was fishing through my briefcase and came across that article. I ended up sitting there and reading for 45 minutes. Then it struck me.

What that article was talking about is *coaching yourself*.

I finally said, 'I have nothing to lose. I'm in trouble, and this might work. I'll give it a try.' I copied a dozen of the ideas into the time organizer book the company gave me."

"Well, I never looked in that section of my organizer again. So the next time, I put the reinforcements on cards. Then somehow I couldn't find the cards. So I went out for another cup of coffee, put the ideas together again—this time on Post-it™ Notes that I stuck on a file folder. Then that night, I unfolded it and read the ideas onto a tape that I use in my car. I figure I can listen to it while I buzz along the freeway heading for my appointments. Who knows? Maybe they'll help somehow."

Noticing a Difference

"Hey, it sounds weak, but I am noticing a difference." Doug laid his jacket over the adjoining chair and sat down. His voice was buoyant and without its usual edge of sarcasm. "Like, when people start acting like turkeys, I think about some of those ideas on my tape. I've stopped saying so many negative things to myself. That makes it easier to deal with the negative things others say to me. I don't use all the ideas yet, but I know my life will be a lot smoother when I do. Listening to those ideas does calm me down and keep me on course. Here are some of my winners:

- When things get tough, I keep coaching myself.
- I can lose the game and still win the championship.
- The playing field doesn't always have to be level.
- It's all right when life isn't fair.
- Doug, you can do it too.

"I still haven't quite gotten to the place where I can accept, 'I talk about my feelings,' but I think I'm getting there. I'm doing other hard things. When I'm driving, I picture myself blocking in my weekly sales plan before four on Friday. I see myself asking for the order and closing. Frankly, this whole idea blows my mind. I didn't think what I said to myself made any difference. I used to think other people were the problem. But I was—well, I guess I was wrong.

"I've discovered that using a self-talk system has helped me. I have a better attitude at work and better communications with my wife. Now, I don't expect my manager to motivate me. That never worked anyway. I know now that my motivation is my responsibility. And these days, when I get home, I go to my wife first, not Goldie. I know that used to bug Brenda. Now I hug her and tell her about my day.

"The other evening she said, 'Doug, what happened? You're not down like you used to be. And you are not talking about turkeys all the time. When you smile now, your eyes smile too.' I could tell by her expression that she really likes what I'm doing. You know, I've been thinking that maybe someday I'll let her listen to my tape."

COACH TALK

Doug started out a doubter and ended up a fan of purposeful self-talk and self-coaching. The principles he learned can be used by all of us to increase our effectiveness and satisfaction in life.

The key principle he discovered was to *coach yourself.* Find the repetition method that works for you, and use it. For some people, the best method may be three-by-five cards, Post-it® Notes, or a computer file. For Doug, it was a cassette tape and his car's tape player.

On his tapes, Doug recorded such "coach talk" as, "You can lose the game and still win the championship," and, "The playing field does not always have to be level."

Here are some other suggestions for coaching yourself:

Most people are fair.

Life has given me a lot.

People have given me a lot.

I keep score on the good things that I have.

When I have a problem with someone, I fix my part of the problem.

I forgive and I move ahead.

I ask for what I want.

I assist people in getting what they want.

I am a most valuable player.

You are a most valuable player.

I find ways to help everyone win.

I ask for the order and I close.

I put papers away right away.

I do it anyway.

I do it now.

WARM-DOWN EXERCISE:

Now it is time to make the transition from Doug's story to your story. As you reflect on Doug's experience, consider these questions:

1. With which parts of the Doug story did you identify?

_____

2. What did you learn or reinforce?

_____

3. After reading Doug's story, what would you be encouraged to do more frequently? (For example: take action rather than waiting for someone to motivate you.)

_____

Your Story

Now, consider these questions about your own story:

1. Assume you are coaching yourself. You are standing alongside the playing field of your daily challenges. As an objective but caring coach, you watch yourself handle the stresses and challenges of life and your career. How would you describe yourself as a player?

_____

2. As your coach, what words of encouragement would you call out?

_____

3. Now, rewrite those words of encouragement into clear, positive statements you can repeat to yourself as reinforcements—that is, as purposeful self-talk you can listen to every day:

_____

One of the primary functions of a coach is to *motivate players* to perseverance and maximum effort in preparation for the game getting tough. It is an important job. So accept the job. Be your own best coach every day. Don't wait for others to change. Make changes where they really count: *within yourself.*

Every time you do this, you will be moving to where you want to be and doing what you want to do.

SECTION WRAP-UP

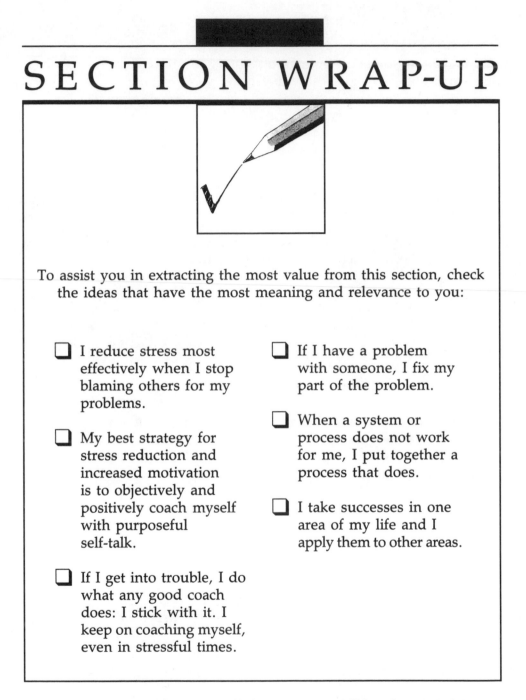

To assist you in extracting the most value from this section, check the ideas that have the most meaning and relevance to you:

❑ I reduce stress most effectively when I stop blaming others for my problems.

❑ My best strategy for stress reduction and increased motivation is to objectively and positively coach myself with purposeful self-talk.

❑ If I get into trouble, I do what any good coach does: I stick with it. I keep on coaching myself, even in stressful times.

❑ If I have a problem with someone, I fix my part of the problem.

❑ When a system or process does not work for me, I put together a process that does.

❑ I take successes in one area of my life and I apply them to other areas.

In the next section, you will discover powerful techniques for an issue practically everyone wants to get in shape—procrastination.

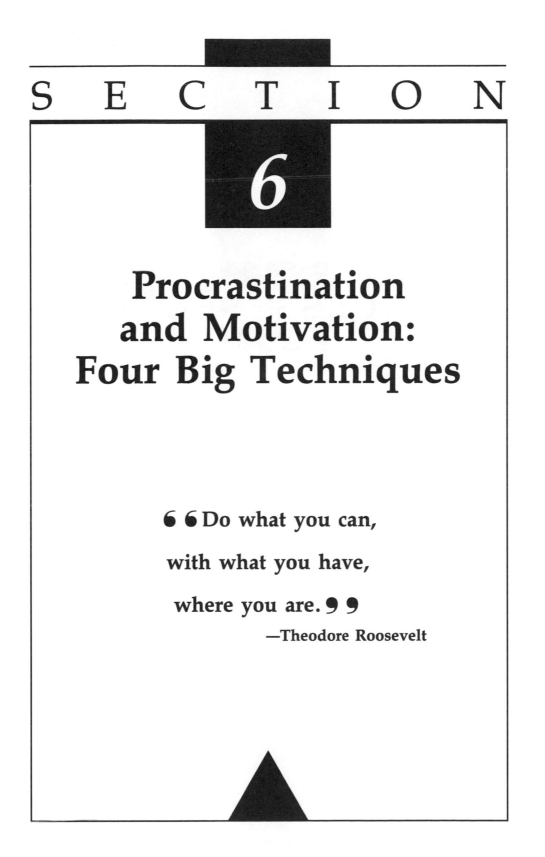

SECTION

6

Procrastination and Motivation: Four Big Techniques

❝Do what you can,

with what you have,

where you are.❞

—Theodore Roosevelt

SUCCESS SECRET

Do it now!

WHO PROCRASTINATES?

The conference room was filled with 500 of the most successful executives and managers in American business. The question raised was, ''How many of you are procrastinating in some area of your life?'' Hands shot up all over the room. At least 400 of the 500 participants answered with a raised hand, Yes, I have a problem with procrastination.

People who procrastinate are not alone. Practically everyone procrastinates on something at some time—even on projects they know will benefit them.

Good News

There is good news in this section for times of procrastination. In the coming pages we will explore practical strategies and shortcuts that have been proven by hundreds of people. We will discover how the guilt and discouragement of procrastination can be transformed into the satisfaction of *getting the right things done*. We will explore:

► Preventing procrastination by coaching yourself with reinforcements (purposeful self-talk).

► Slaying the procrastination menace with four super techniques.

PROCRASTINATION PREVENTION AND SELF-TALK

Take a closer look at the first of these powerful techniques for procrastination-proofing yourself.

Procrastination-Proofing Technique #1:
Grab 15

This classic technique for overcoming procrastination heads the popularity list every time. You will be amazed at what you can accomplish by working on a job at least fifteen minutes a day.

For most people the hardest part of conquering procrastination is *getting started.* When you promise yourself that your commitment is for only fifteen minutes, it's much easier to get started. One man even made one of his reinforcements: ''I can do anything for fifteen minutes!''

Consider what you can accomplish by consistently investing fifteen minutes a day:

- Write a manual
- Remodel a room
- Catch up on paperwork
- Grow a small garden
- Flatten your stomach

- Learn a new language in three years
- Read the entire Bible in a year
- Learn a new computer application
- Learn to read financial reports

Charlotte Hale Allen saw tangible proof of this powerful technique when she and her husband visited a friend in a small southern town. Their friend was the town's only doctor and the new owner of a rambling house that had been vacant for years. When they arrived, their friend was standing in the middle of a room with paint cans and tools scattered across the floor. He looked at the ceiling and declared, ''That has got to come down.'' They thought he was merely dreaming until he took them into his new bathroom. The ceiling was lowered. New cabinets were installed. New plumbing was in place. He smiled as he pointed with pride to the heated towel bar he had installed.

When they asked how he did it, he smiled again and said, ''It's simple. I work at least fifteen minutes a day, every day, without fail.''

Grab 15 can help you tackle those projects at work that have been falling behind.

The Computer and Grab 15

Here is good news for all the people who have not learned to use their computer applications. Put the Grab 15 technique to work. You can become quite proficient with a blitz study of only fifteen minutes each day. One computer whiz explained her success. ''I learned a command a day. That's all it took.'' Those few minutes a day add up.

15 Minutes a Day Equals 78 Hours a Year

Here's the secret of the Grab 15 technique:

Fifteen minutes a day, day after day, quickly adds up. Even if you take Sunday off, you can chalk up 90 productive minutes a week. Just look:

15 minutes × 6 days = 90 minutes a week

90 minutes a week × 52 weeks = 4,680 minutes or 78 hours.

Imagine what you could accomplish if someone waved a wand and magically gave you 78 extra hours! The Grab 15 technique puts that magic wand in your own hands! Here are some of the added benefits of the Grab 15 technique:

The Creativity Benefit

When you work on a task for fifteen minutes a day, that task is always simmering on the back burner of your mind. Imagine walking into a kitchen where there is a pan of spiced apple cider on the stove gently heating on the back burner. The aroma is everywhere. So is your creativity when you commit to Grab 15. Even when you are not consciously thinking about the job, your subconscious is working for you. You discover unexpected resources and new ways to streamline your tasks. You think and work more creatively.

The Bonus Benefit

Some days, after you finish your fifteen-minute commitment, you will be on a roll. You will feel like continuing. And you will. That bonus effort will bring you that much closer to your goal.

Add to your motivation by telling yourself: ''I Grab 15.''

Exercise:

Test it yourself!

1. Pick a big job that is sliding behind schedule, or any task of any size for which you have not been able to find time.

2. Commit yourself to working on that task at least fifteen minutes a day. Think about it: When is the best time of day to carve out that fifteen minutes?

3. Consider how you can reward yourself for your consistency. It could be anything from a star on your calendar to a gift for yourself, perhaps a book you've been wanting to read, or a CD you have been wanting to enjoy.

Procrastination-Proofing Technique #2: Do the Toughest Top Priority First

---

Tackle that important but unpleasant task first and get it out of the way. Have you ever had a day when, as you drive to work, you are thinking about that job that *has* to be done, but that job is the *last* thing you want to do? Have you noticed that the longer you put it off, the more it haunts you and will not let you forget it? It hovers over you like a gray cloud. If you move away from your desk, it follows you. When the phone rings, you hope it is not someone wondering if that tough top-priority job is done.

Now picture this: As you drive to work, you think about that tough top-priority task and you flex your mental muscles. Arriving at your desk, you meet that task head-on. It may be that report you have been putting off, that bad news phone call you need to make, that correspondence you need to answer. Whatever it is, as soon as you get it done, the whole world lights up. That gray cloud floats away. You feel your life is under control. You feel energized!

Is there something on your mind right now that needs to be done, but you don't feel like doing it? If so, give it a name:

_____

Next, give yourself a lift. Picture yourself getting that job done and out of your life.

Now, make that picture a reality. Tackle that job *now*.

Procrastination-Proofing Technique #3: Keep Your Stimulation and Excitement Quota Full

Many people procrastinate because they thrive on the challenge of getting things done under last-minute pressure. The individual with a High Stimulation and Excitement Quota regularly ends up getting things done at the last minute. If it is 8:00 A.M. and he has a report due at 4:00 P.M. and the report preparation takes an hour, you can predict that he will start on the report at 3:00 P.M. Or maybe 3:15. It is more exciting that way. If a person with a High Stimulation and Excitement Quota inadvertently gets caught up on her work before a trip or an event, she will feel compelled to add a new project.

If you identify with the High Stimulation and Excitement Quota, you can read an entire chapter on this dynamic in *How to Put More Time in Your Life* by Dru Scott.

The solution is to keep your Stimulation and Excitement Quota filled productively. This reduces the need to fill your Quota by procrastination. If you know you like a lot of excitement, plan for it. Lunch with a new person, take on a new assignment, join an extra professional association, learn a new software application. You know what appeals to your personality. Keep your S&EQ at the level you want. Reinforce yourself with:

- I plan for a good amount of excitement in my life.
- I keep my Stimulation and Excitement Quota filled in positive ways.

Procrastination-Proofing Technique #4: Face Up to the Feeling

Procrastination can be a way of avoiding feelings—most often feelings of success, enjoyment, or closeness. Many people procrastinate to avoid the feeling they would have if they finished the task—not just to avoid the task itself. You may want to read more details about procrastination and feelings in *How to Put More Time in Your Life*. Consider how these statements could show up in procrastination:

- I wouldn't know what to do if I got caught up.
- If I got caught up on my work, it would scare me to death.
- I feel needed when I have a lot of work to do.

If you see some connections, consider using these self-talk reinforcements:

- I accept what I am feeling without trying to cover it with work.
- My feelings are OK.
- I talk about my feelings because that helps me control them.
- It is OK for me to feel (name the feeling you may be avoiding).

Pick the procrastination techniques that reduce stress and build your motivation.

SECTION WRAP-UP

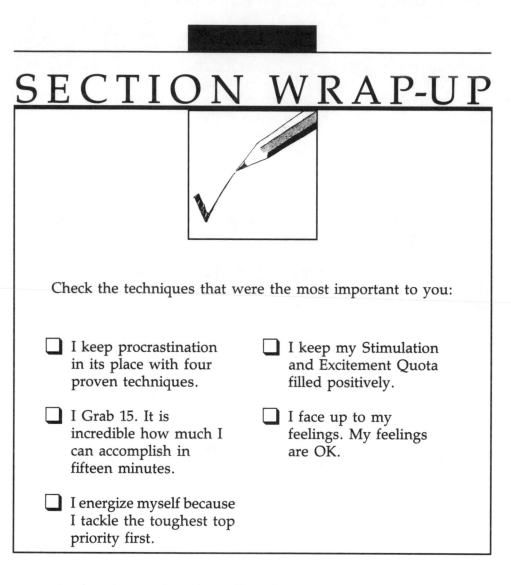

Check the techniques that were the most important to you:

❏ I keep procrastination in its place with four proven techniques.

❏ I Grab 15. It is incredible how much I can accomplish in fifteen minutes.

❏ I energize myself because I tackle the toughest top priority first.

❏ I keep my Stimulation and Excitement Quota filled positively.

❏ I face up to my feelings. My feelings are OK.

In the next section you will explore a powerful system to motivate yourself. The system will help you generate motivation beyond your fondest dreams!

SECTION

7

Mega Motivation with Pictures of Excellence

66 Where there is no vision

the people perish. 99

—Proverbs 29:18

SUCCESS SECRET

Since we are motivated
by what we are missing,
why not put this reality to work.

Picture what you want
in wonderful detail.

WE ARE MOTIVATED BY WHAT WE ARE MISSING

"I have the best nose money can buy," Teri explained as she chuckled and slipped off her glasses so everyone in the seminar could get a good look at her nose. A woman in her early forties with light brown hair and laughing eyes, she went on, "You talk about being motivated by what you are missing. I am an example. I have a beautiful nose now, but this is not my original nose."

Teri by a Nose

"You should have seen me when I was in school," she explained. "As soon as I started first grade, I became self-conscious about my nose. It was big with a definite hook. Kids in my class called me 'The Beak' and 'Honker.' If I were to show you my school pictures, you'd see why the kids teased me. It was a *major* nose!

"Throughout my school years, it was all I thought about. I wore long bangs in a futile attempt to detract from it. I begged to wear glasses. I did everything I could to make my nose less noticeable. I used to dream what it would be like to have a small nose. I imagined striding into a room, shoulders back, chin up, flashing my new nose.

"Finally, when I was 25, my husband and I agreed I was going to have cosmetic surgery. At last, I was going to have the nose I had imagined for so many years. After the surgery, the doctor removed the bandages from my nose. I looked in the mirror. I could see that the skin was still tender and red, but I knew my nose was going to be beautiful! It was exactly the size and shape I had dreamed about since I was a kid!

"Only moments later as I held the mirror and admired my nose, I saw something that I had never, ever noticed before. Not my nose—my *teeth*. For the first time, I noticed the gap between my two front teeth. It had always been there, but I never paid attention to it until I got my nose fixed! My dream of a beautiful nose had come true—yet within seconds, I forgot the nose I had been obsessed with for almost twenty years! Now, all I was thinking about was that gap between my two front teeth!"

Teri's story is an example of this reality: We are motivated by what we are missing.

MOTIVATIONAL POWER WITH PICTURES

How can you put this reality to work? Develop a *picture* in your mind. You want that missing promotion. You picture yourself at your new desk, dealing with your new responsibilities, collecting that new, bigger paycheck.

We can *harness* the pulling power of mental pictures to motivate us toward our achievable goals. The way to harness the power of these pictures is by learning to *picture what you want in vivid detail*. There is unbelievable motivating power in imagining ''pictures of excellence.''

Turning your targets, objectives and dreams into pictures of excellence helps you *miss* them. Picturing the finished result you want triggers the *missing* effect and adds to your motivation. Expressing the results you desire in pictures gives you an extra supply of drive and discipline. Here are some examples:

Picture of Excellence #1: Jerry—Jerry, a do-it-yourself carpenter in his spare time, pictures the family room addition he wants to build on his house, and he imagines it in great detail: comfortable couch in front of a stone fireplace, a big-screen TV in the corner, his three children laughing and munching popcorn as they enjoy the spacious new addition.

Picture of Excellence #2: Devona—Devona keeps herself motivated in her sales engineering job by picturing that high-end, high-tech packaging system already installed and running in her customer's plant. She sees her customer's employees standing beside the system, measuring how rapidly it runs and how much time and money it is saving.

Picture of Excellence #3: Barbara—Barbara pictures herself at her goal weight. She is standing in front of a mirror wearing a red dress in size 7.

Picture of Excellence #4: Gary—Gary fuels his motivation as human resources manager of a 5,000-employee company by picturing people coming to work with smiles. He envisions the main gate on a Monday morning. His employees stream through the gate, talking to each other about how they can do an even better job. ''When we are doing our job as managers,'' he says, ''people will be smiling as they come to work. This picture makes it easy to challenge each manager toward excellence in employee relations.''

These different people in different situations make their lives more satisfying and their organizations more effective by picturing what they want. Detailed pictures of excellence put enormous motivational power in our heads and in our hands. They encourage us to take action.

Why Do Pictures of Excellence Work So Powerfully?

1. Providing Right-Brain Involvement

Pictures involve the visual, spatial, creative properties of the right brain, not just the cognitive properties of the left brain. So often statements of purpose and direction appeal only to left brain. Pictures of excellence add the power appeal of the right-brain hemisphere.

2. Giving Your Objectives the Appeal of the Emotional First Brain

There is some exciting new information which shows that pictures directly affect our more primitive brain first even before they reach the left and right hemispheres. In Bert Decker's book, *You've Got To Be Believed To Be Heard*, he talks about the *First Brain*, which is our emotional brain (the limbic system). It is that primitive and unconscious part of the brain that is a powerful driving force in our lives. The First Brain is directly affected by all of our sensory input. What you see and hear is literally transmitted through the First Brain even before it reaches the left and right hemispheres of the "New Brain," the cerebral cortex. Although the First Brain is affected by all senses, it is very much dominated by the visual input. Which is why visualizing pictures can have an even more powerful impact than ever thought possible.

So, traditionally, if a leader wanted to communicate the organization's goals to the "troops," he or she used words, logic, rationales, facts and analyses designed to appeal to the thinking brain (cerebral cortex). The facts and figures reach only the conscious and reach only the left side of the conscious brain at that. It is easy to see why so many people lose interest and nod during traditional meetings.

Facts and logic inform; they do not inspire. They do not excite. They do not activate our emotional brain. However, paint a picture and you add the pulling power of the emotional First Brain.

Using Word Pictures As Reinforcements

Actual pictures work the best, but not everyone can draw or has an actual picture. You may need to "draw" the picture with words before you can see it in your mind. Then when you say the words, the picture flashes onto the screen of your mind.

A GREAT PLACE TO WORK

You can use word pictures to focus your team or organization on achieving a common goal. Here are two ways pictures can motivate and make your organization a great place to work.

1. Teamwork with Shared Pictures of Excellence

When you help your group visualize a picture that represents group success, you give people a priceless gift: *direction and motivation.* Often, goals and objectives come across to employees as a collection of cold words and numbing figures. A vivid, detailed picture of excellence plants a common vision of success in the minds of everyone. It unifies them and pulls them in the same direction. Groups move forward more rapidly when their leaders unite them around a shared picture of where the group is going. Leadership means communicating a shared picture of excellence.

- Bill, the head of an information systems department, inspires his staff with this word picture: ''Imagine a group of company people around a table discussing a decision. Thanks to us, that group has the right information at the right time in the right form at the right place.''

- Mary, the vice president of a 600-bed medical center, shares this word picture with her nursing staff: ''A man is leaving our out-patient treatment facility and he is saying to the person picking him up, 'The people at the medical center are wonderful. They gave me great care and there were no surprises.' ''

2. Self-Management with Shared Pictures of Excellence

When each person in a group can picture and describe where your group wants to go, you encourage self-management. People make better decisions when they know why and where they are going. A big reason for poor decisions, lack of motivation and lack of initiative is that people do not clearly understand where the group is going and why.

- Janet pictures her manufacturing plant site with the new distillation tower completed and operating.

- Howard pictures the quality process implemented so solidly in his organization that people have taped on the wall in each work group two or three scoreboards of key measurements.

Exercise: Check Out the Group's Pictures

At your next group meeting, ask each person to write down a few words that describe what your group will be doing and looking like when the group is successful a year from now. Then compare pictures. You may want to do it again with a three-year time frame.

THREE SUCCESS SECRETS

1. Make Them Snapshot Specific

To gain motivational value, fill your word pictures with vivid detail. Make them as specific as an actual photograph.

2. Find a Word Picture for Each Priority Area

If an area of your life is important to you, find a picture to represent where you want to go with it.

- If you're working on a cost-reduction program, picture the pizza party to celebrate reaching your cost-reduction goals.

- If you want a strong marriage, find a picture that represents what you will be doing and enjoying in your strong marriage. Perhaps sitting at a table discussing problems and working out solutions. Or picture going out to a candlelight dinner for a special date with your marriage partner.

Exercise: The Picture Gallery in Your Mind

To get the most motivational power, write a word picture for each of your five or six priority areas on the job and at home. Use your word pictures as the basis for your gallery of mental pictures of excellence.

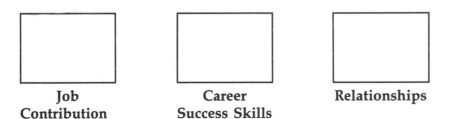

| Job Contribution | Career Success Skills | Relationships |

3. Refresh Them Daily

If you put your objectives and plans in a dusty file, they will not help you. It is the same with your pictures of excellence. A picture without daily refreshing. Include your word pictures in your reinforcements. Think of them morning and evening. If they are of special importance or difficulty, think about them two or three additional times throughout the day. Here is a bonus idea. Experiment with dedicating your time waiting on the phone to review your pictures of excellence.

Remember the first time you were in love. Chances are you didn't have any trouble finding time to think about the object of your affection. Use the same persistence for refreshing the pictures you want to achieve. Let them stimulate your creativity and action.

SECTION WRAP-UP

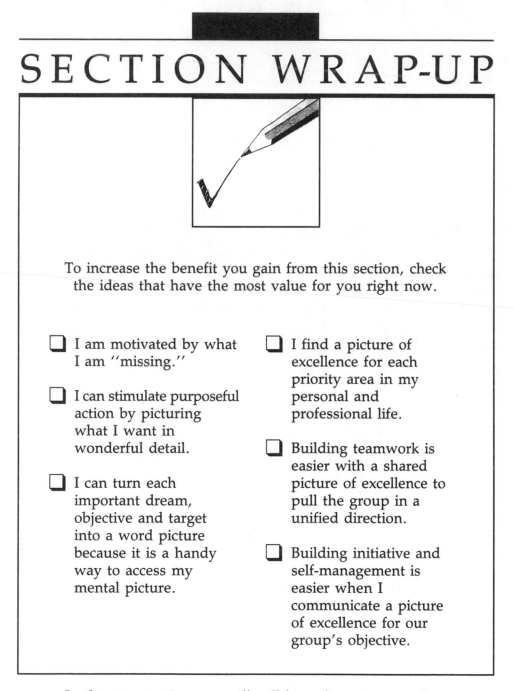

To increase the benefit you gain from this section, check the ideas that have the most value for you right now.

☐ I am motivated by what I am "missing."

☐ I can stimulate purposeful action by picturing what I want in wonderful detail.

☐ I can turn each important dream, objective and target into a word picture because it is a handy way to access my mental picture.

☐ I find a picture of excellence for each priority area in my personal and professional life.

☐ Building teamwork is easier with a shared picture of excellence to pull the group in a unified direction.

☐ Building initiative and self-management is easier when I communicate a picture of excellence for our group's objective.

In the next section you will will learn how to steer clear of reinforcement pitfalls so that you focus totally on reinforcements that work!

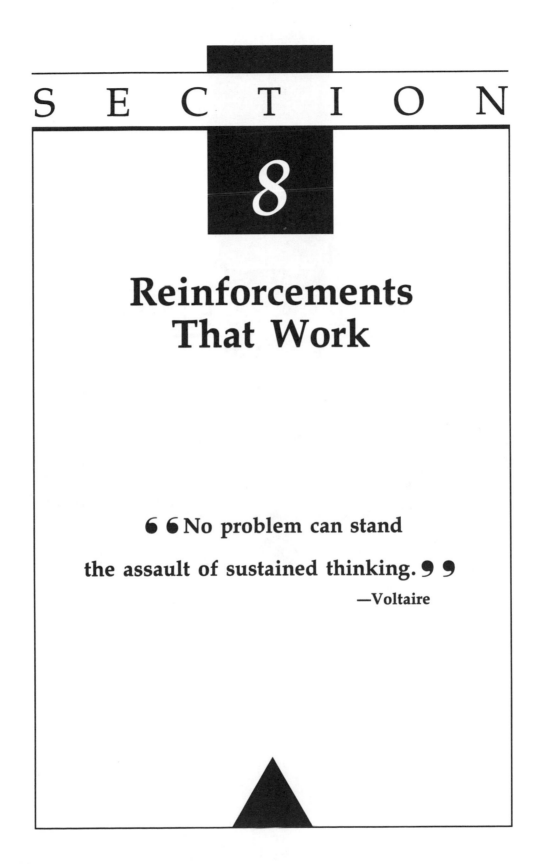

SECTION

8

Reinforcements That Work

" No problem can stand

the assault of sustained thinking. "

—Voltaire

SUCCESS SECRET

Reinforce the best

THE RIGHT REINFORCEMENTS FOR YOU

Matt still looked like a football player, although he had not played in years. As he glanced at the group around the conference table, he attested "The area where I need to improve? I don't even have to think about it. My problem is listening. When people talk to me, I'm practicing my response rather than hearing what they are saying. On Saturday my wife told me again that she could barely get the words out of her mouth before I tossed in a solution. On Monday a man at work told me that I didn't listen. I got hit with that twice in three days. My back was to the wall. I decided I had to change from being a mouth to an ear."

In Matt's campaign to use his ears more than his mouth, his first draft of reinforcements sounded like this:

> I am going to listen better.
> Listening is not a waste of time.
> People think I am a good listener.

He then shaped them into more workable reinforcements:

> I score with listening.
> I enjoy listening and I learn a lot.
> I listen for facts and feelings.

Matt produced winning reinforcements because he:

- Picked the key arena he wanted to improve
- Tapped into the power of reinforcements that are Present, Positive, Personal, Playful and Challenging

Your Growing Edge

Reinforcements need to fit you. You will get the best results with the right reinforcements for *your* personality, *your* priorities, and *your* problems. So what are fast ways to make sure you have the right topics in your self-talk reinforcement system?

First of all, pick the areas where you want to accomplish more and contribute more—your pictures of excellence, targets and objectives. Put together a strong offense. Then pay attention to any barriers that stand in your way in those areas. These reinforcements give you a good defense.

When you use reinforcements that are written skillfully, they prompt you to take the action you want. Consistently. So make sure your reinforcements work for you.

THE FIVE BIGGEST TRAPS IN SELF-TALK

If you hear someone say, "I tried it once and it didn't work," turn on the red warning light. He has probably been handed some self-talk statements with defects. The defects and traps are common. Watch out for them.

The following chart reveals those five big traps plus how you can steer clear of each one.

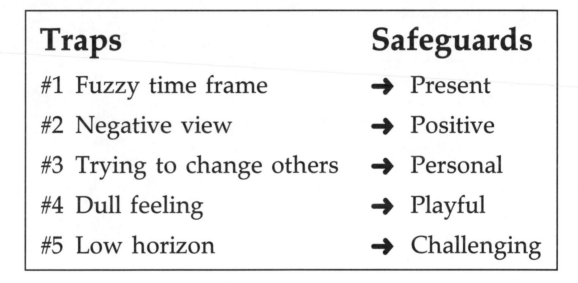

Traps	Safeguards
#1 Fuzzy time frame	→ Present
#2 Negative view	→ Positive
#3 Trying to change others	→ Personal
#4 Dull feeling	→ Playful
#5 Low horizon	→ Challenging

The Most Important Three

The first three—Present, Positive and Personal—are the most important safeguards; the last two add zest and excitement. Now, let's look at some examples that will help you make sure you have reinforcements that work for you.

FIVE SAFEGUARDS

#1 Safeguard: *Present*

Reinforcements are best stated as a present belief, not as a hoped-for future attainment. They are designed to enhance behavior today. Using "will" delays the benefit.

Replace: I will Grab 15.

Use: *I Grab 15.*

Replace: We will get feedback from our customers on how well we are meeting requirements.

Use: *We get feedback from our customers on how well we are meeting requirements.*

The purpose of reinforcements is to get our present behavior to conform to our new beliefs. Our minds tend to put off implementing reinforcements that are stated in the future tense.

Exercise:

Rewrite these statements bringing them into the present.

1. I will do it now.

_____

2. I am going to lose weight.

_____

3. Some day I am going to get a job where I can contribute.

_____

4. I am going to get these references organized.

_____

5. I am going to start talking to people about opportunities in my organization.

_____

FIVE SAFEGUARDS (continued)

#2 Safeguard: *Positive*

This is the *rear-view mirror problem.* Someone who says to himself, ''I don't procrastinate,'' is looking at past performance and also at negative performance. It is like looking in the rear-view mirror at where you have been, rather than looking at where you want to be.

Replace: I don't procrastinate.

Use: *I do it now.*

Replace: I am never over budget.

Use: *I am always on budget.*

Since our word pictures and self-talk have such pulling power, do not let them pull you backward. Just as we do not drive while looking in the rear-view mirror; do not train your mind by looking at where you do not want to be. Move ahead with reinforcements that are positive.

Exercise:

Rewrite these statements and weave in the positive.

1. No more time spent hunting. No more lost items.

   _____

2. I'm not going to go to pieces.

   _____

3. I don't have defects in my work.

   _____

4. I don't have any difficult people at work.

   _____

5. I'm always running behind at work.

   _____

#3 Safeguard: *Personal*

The best reinforcements reflect our role in achieving our own targets and objectives. The most useful focus is on changing ourselves, not others.

Replace: They don't appreciate me.

Use: *I ask for what I want.*

Replace: You'll never make it.

Use: *You can do it too.*

We are not responsible for what others do to us, how others treat us, or whether others appreciate us. We are responsible for ourselves. This personal, self-responsibility focus needs to be reflected in the say our reinforcements are written.

Exercise: Work Through the Following Statements to Make Them Personal.

1. They should know what I want.

   _____

2. I am just waiting until someone notices.

   _____

3. I shouldn't have to tell them.

   _____

4. My boss should motivate me.

   _____

5. You can't do it.

   _____

Now that you have worked through the practice statements for Present, Positive and Personal, take a look at the sample answers on the next page.

CHECK YOUR REWRITES

Are your rewrites close to these? Use these as ideas only. There are many ways to improve the sample statements.

1. Present examples

1. I do it now.

2. I see myself weighing my goal weight.

3. I am making a solid contribution in my job.

4. I have well-organized references.

5. I talk to people every day about opportunities in my organization.

2. Positive examples

1. No temporary parking places. I put it in place or in use.

2. I take care of my needs and wants in positive ways. I take some purposeful action and I feel better.

3. I produce work that is defect free, on time, every time.

4. I am on time and frequently early. I get a kick out of getting things done in advance.

3. Personal examples

1. I ask for what I want from people who can give it to me.

2. I let people know what I have accomplished.

3. I ask directly.

4. I read my reinforcements daily. I put together pictures of excellence and processes to get there.

5. You can do it too.

Now, lets look at Safeguards #4 and #5: Playful and Challenging.

SAFEGUARDS 4 AND 5

#4 Safeguard: *Playful*

Each of us has more energy and commitment when life is fun. You will be more effective when you sprinkle some playfulness into your reinforcements. For example,

Replace: I do not stop until I have finished a task.

Use: *I finish fully, and I feel great.*

Replace: I weigh my goal weight.

Use: *I love bouncing over to that scale and it shows my goal weight.*

Replace: I see myself taking the stairs at work.

Use: *I enjoy seeing myself bounding up those stairs at work.*

#5 Safeguard: *Challenging*

We are not inspired by getting by, just surviving or by not going bankrupt. We are motivated by the plus side—doing well, achieving financial freedom, feeling good or earning an award at work.

Replace: I just want to get through the day.

Use: *I turn problems into opportunities.*

Replace: I want to have enough money to pay the bills.

Use: *I do things every day to achieve financial freedom.*

Replace: I just hope my customers don't call about these problems.

Use: *I get the specifics so we can prevent problems.*

The most energizing reinforcements encourage productive action. They give you a mental pat on the back and a look in the right direction. They communicate, ''You can do it! And the time to do it is now!''

Replace Rather Than Try to Remove

It is difficult to remove old messages that do not work. Once you recognize them, outnumber them with a flood of constructive reinforcements.

FINE TUNING YOUR MENTAL BACKGROUND MUSIC

As you listen to what you say to yourself, think: "I am interested in honestly hearing the messages I repeat to myself. If I am saying some things that drag me down, I want to recognize them. If I am saying things that direct and lift, I want to appreciate them." Turn up the volume. Listen closely to yourself. You may be surprised at what you learn.

Childhood Messages Are Still on the Job Today

As you tune into messages that are bouncing around your mind, be aware of when you learned the messages. Many were picked up when you were a child. Today these messages still have a powerful influence on who we are and what we do.

Much of the growth we want to experience involves replacing habits, patterns and messages we learned in childhood. This is not an indictment of parents. Our parents did the best they could with what they had.

One goal of purposeful self-talk is to re-parent and re-coach ourselves along even more productive patterns and toward more meaningful goals, which we as self-responsible and self-directed adults consciously choose.

Exercise: Tune in to the Messages You Learned in Childhood

Since the messages we say to ourselves have so much impact, they deserve some discovery time. To jump-start your thought processes, look over the following list. What messages did you learn about each of these topics? Jot down the first ideas that come to your mind. If nothing occurs to you about a particular topic, skip it and go on.

Being successful	Working
Making a lot of money	Hard work
Being famous	Relaxing
Getting what you want	Where you would end up
Being happy	Who you would be like
Your name	Making decisions
Your nicknames	Overcoming obstacles
Education	Getting ahead
Pressure	

AS DESTRUCTIVE AS STICKS AND STONES

As a child, you probably heard ''sticks and stones may break my bones, but names will never hurt me.'' The fact is that name-calling can and does hurt us all the time. Consider the following questions:

- Did anyone ever call you names as a child or adolescent? How do you feel about those names right now as you recall them?

- Most importantly, do you ever call yourself those names?

Peel Off Those Labels—Some people call themselves ''stupid,'' ''crazy,'' ''bad,'' ''failure'' or ''ugly.'' For example, ''I'm bad. I didn't do the report on time.'' That is a negative label. It drills into a person a sense of defeat and condemnation. This kind of label doesn't help anyone. A positive label works much better. Or the person could rewrite this statement to make it constructive and motivating. ''I did not do the report on time. I have solved problems like this before, and I am taking action right now to solve this one and to prevent it in the future.'' A rule of thumb for negative labels:

- Change them to positive labels or
- Change them to a description with encouragement to take purposeful action.

Exercise:

Think about your use of labels and names to describe yourself. What specifically do you say to yourself when you:

- Make a mistake?
- Get angry?
- Are corrected?
- Do not get what you want?

Do any of the labels or messages need to be updated? If so, which ones?

_____

As you think of new and better things to say to yourself, consider weaving in these principles:

- Describe without labeling
- Solve problems without blaming yourself or others
- Prevent problems

Go ahead and write the new reinforcements that will serve you more effectively.

_____

REINFORCEMENTS THAT ENCOURAGE

Many people did not hear the appreciation and encouragement they wanted and needed as a child. This person often feels frustrated with others on the job. As an adult, it is tempting for this individual to expect people at work to give them what they missed when there were growing up.

As adults we can fill this gap. First, remember that our parents did the best they could with what they had. This clears away resentment. Second, include the missing reinforcements.

Great resources for this special coaching and reinforcements are the research and work of Robert M. Goulding, M.D. and Mary McClure Goulding, M.S.W. You will find solid ideas in their books: *Redecision Therapy* and their latest book, *Not To Worry*. Buy them both. You will find them most informative.

Replace: I can't ever win.

Use: *I am on my way!*

Replace: I am never good enough.

Use: *Of course I am a success!*

Replace: I don't feel important.

Use: *Of course I am important.*

Replace: I always feel like an outsider.

Use: *Make room for me.*

Replace: I never was a kid.

Use: *It's not too late for a happy childhood.*

Replace: There's something wrong with me.

Use: *I am all right the way I am.*

Reinforcements that encourage are powerful tools. Use the ones that work for you.

SECTION WRAP-UP

To help you build habits of listening to your self-talk
and rewriting your messages that do not work into
messages that do, check the concepts from this section
that you found the most helpful:

❏ I steer clear of five
pitalls: the fuzzy time
frame, negativeness,
trying to change others,
dull feeling and too low
of a horizon.

❏ Purposeful action in my
focus. The best
reinforcements prompt
me to take action in the
right direction.

❏ I make sure my
reinforcements are:
present, positive,
personal, playful and
challenging.

In the next section, you will get to know a woman who stepped
out and overcame tremendous obstacles by consistently
and persistently using pictures of excellence.

SECTION

9

Persistence, Pictures and a Happy Ending

❝The future belongs to those who believe in the beauty of their dreams.❞

—Eleanor Roosevelt

SUCCESS SECRET

Persistence pays.

Keep on picturing what you want
in wonderful detail.

BARBARA'S SUCCESS STORY

Success stories widen our horizons and inspire us to keep on moving toward our own dreams. Every once in a while a story does more. It touches a deeper chord. It says in undeniable ways "You can do it too!" Such is the story of Barbara.

The results in the following case story of Barbara are so dramatic that they almost seem unbelievable. Yet Barbara's story is true. The results she achieved are real. Barbara is someone who had every right in the world to say, "I tried it once and it didn't work." But Barbara is living proof that the path to achievement is paved with persistence.

A Solid Foundation

You will understand Barbara's story better when you know that she had built a foundation. For six years, she had attended weekly meetings in a Twelve Step program. In working the steps, she had developed the habit of mentally reinforcing helpful beliefs day by day. In addition, for four years, she had invested in family therapy for herself and her two children. Here are Barbara's own words as she spoke to the group in a follow up seminar.

Barbara's Case Story

"My life reads like 'The Perils of Pauline!'" confessed Barbara. A "thirty-something" brunette with a penchant for self-deprecation, Barbara was desperate, depressed, and seventy pounds overweight. She made jokes at her own expense, such as: "I go to the tent section to buy my dresses. And I always avoid bridges. Their load limit is ten tons."

With surprising frankness, Barbara shared her story: Divorced after seventeen years of marriage to a physically and mentally abusive alcoholic, Barbara was convinced she was a loser. Illness and misery stalked her constantly. When her husband discontinued child support, she and her two children moved in with her mother. "And that," she added, "was no day at the beach"

Four Packs of Cigarettes and Nine Bouts of Pneumonia

Barbara smoked four packs of cigarettes a day in spite of nine bouts with pneumonia and pleurisy. When doctors discovered signs of emphysema, she stopped smoking and her weight gain began. A routine exam revealed a tumor on her thyroid. Surgery confirmed it was malignant. Barbara underwent radiation treatment and gained more weight. Meanwhile, her father and a close friend died of lung cancer.

BARBARA'S SUCCESS STORY (continued)

"I was miserable most of the time," she admitted. "I was convinced I was going to die. I figured cancer was everywhere. You feel as if your body has turned against you. You're only buying time."

She even made out her will and tagged little Post-it™ Notes to her possessions, with the names of those who were to inherit each item after she died. Weeks passed, and Barbara was actually surprised to find that she was still alive, even though her doctors assured her the malignancy was being controlled and had not spread.

"I Can't Go Out Tonight. I Have Cancer."

Barbara returned to work—an administrative position—and resumed her life. At about this time, she received a phone call from a man she had dated years before. "Hi, Barbara," he said. "I hear you're divorced now. I was wondering if you'd like to go out."

"Oh, no, I'm sorry," said Barbara. "I've gotten really fat and I don't date."

"It doesn't have to be a date. How about just going out for a drink?"

"I'm sorry, but I don't drink."

"Well, you say you're really fat, so you must eat. Would you like to go out for dinner?"

"No, I don't think so. I've been through a terrible trauma with my divorce and I'm not quite over it yet."

"Really? How long have you been divorced?"

"Three and a half years."

A few weeks later another man called and asked her out to a movie. She said, "Oh, thank you, but I can't. I have cancer."

Dead silence.

Losing a Gymnast

''Those conversations show what my mental attitude was like,'' Barbara explained to the group. ''Everything focused on my being sick. Every morning I'd wake up, hit the snooze alarm seven times, drag myself to the shower, and by the time I yanked my panty hose on, I was so tired and out of breath I had to sit down and rest.

''I didn't walk anywhere. Even though my office was only two buildings away from the cafeteria, I drove to lunch every day. Every night after work, I put on my pajamas, took my dinner upstairs to my bed, and spent the evening eating and watching TV. I lived that way for years.

''Finally, my doctor told me I had to lose 77 pounds. That was the year of the Olympics when media attention was focused on Mary Lou Retton. She weighed 78 pounds. I thought: The doctor wants me to lose a small gymnast! How in the world can I do it?!

Self-Fulfilling Prophecies

''About this time, I attended my first seminar. The trainer handed out packets of preprinted blue cards to everybody. Each of those cards contained a positive statement, such as:

- I concentrate.
- I turn problems into opportunities.
- I picture what I want to accomplish in wonderful detail.

''The trainer explained, 'If you put positive reinforcements in your mind, your behavior will gradually change to reflect what your mind believes to be true.'''

''I was intrigued. Could it really be true that you are what you tell yourself you are? I realized that my self-talk was absolutely terrible! I was always telling myself, 'I'm tired. I don't feel good. I'm sick. I'm stupid. I can't win.' A whole string of self-sabotaging, self-fulfilling prophecies. Sure, I believed in positive thinking. I just figured it only worked for people who were already positive. After listening to the trainer, I thought I might actually be able to change and become a positive person myself!

''Next, the trainer handed out blank cards and told us to write down our wishes or desires—and to state them as positive affirmations. She said, 'If you want to lose weight, write down what you want to weigh. For example, 'I am a 120-pound woman. I picture myself at my goal weight.'

BARBARA'S SUCCESS STORY (continued)

''Well, that got my attention!

''But I was skeptical too. Easy for her to say this self-talk works. She's cute, thin and smart. She travels all around the world and she's financially independent. She probably has a husband who's thin, cute and smart too!''

Doing It Anyway

But Barbara dutifully wrote out her reinforcements—statements that expressed a belief in the future possibilities to conquer present realities. ''I was 70 pounds overweight when I wrote out the card that said, 'I am a 120–pound woman.' I was snacking on spaghetti and garlic bread when I wrote, 'I love raw vegetables. If I am tempted to graze, I reach for the raw veggies.' I was out of breath after getting dressed in the morning when I wrote, 'I walk a mile a day.' Those reinforcements contrasted so wildly with the way I really lived that I could hardly bring myself to read the cards.''

Barbara took the cards home despite her skepticism. ''I showed my mother,'' she said. ''Actually I would have liked to have brought her a stack too!'' Barbara put the cards on her nightstand, intending to start building some good self-talk habits into her life. Instead, the cards collected dust for the next three months.

''One Saturday morning on my way to work, I stopped at Bagels and Doughnuts and bought a dozen doughnuts—two of which were eclairs. I planned to have a few doughnuts at work, then take the rest home. By 3 in the afternoon, that doughnut box was completely empty. Of the two other people who were there, only one had eaten a doughnut. I realized I had eaten all the rest myself! That evening I went out to dinner with a friend. I had a big meal at Howard Johnson's and topped it off with a maple-walnut sundae. I went home feeling absolutely miserable.

A Turning Point

''That was a turning point in my thinking. I felt like Scarlet in *Gone With The Wind* when she raised her arm skyward and swore that she would never be poor again. In my bedroom that night, I raised my arm upward and I swore, 'I have had it! I swear, as God is in heaven, I will never be fat again!''''

''That night,'' she recalled, ''I was lying in bed when I noticed those cards from the seminar. I picked them up in desperation. The doctor had ordered me to lose 77 pounds, but nothing worked. I figured I had nothing to lose—or should I say everything to lose—so I decided to read those cards. I even wrote another card that said: I walk a mile a day. I could hardly write those words.

''The next day I pulled on my sweat suit and drove to the track in a park near home. Somehow, I made it around the track even though I had to sit and rest on the bench at each quarter-mile.

''I kept on reading my cards faithfully every day, morning and evening, for one month. And at the end of 30 days, exactly nothing happened.

''My seminar leader had guaranteed that I would get results if I would read the cards for 60 days. So I kept on reading every morning and evening.

An Amazing Discovery

Barbara continued to read her reinforcement cards faithfully every day. ''After five weeks, I found them so powerful,'' she maintained, ''I knew I would have to make changes in my life or stop reading the cards. *My mind wanted to do what the cards said I was doing.* Day after day, I kept reading my cards and picturing myself at my goal weight. I pictured my hand reaching into the refrigerator and picking up a handful of carrots rather than the cold spaghetti. I kept picturing myself walking around the track. By this time, I was walking four miles every evening instead of watching TV. After seven weeks, I made an amazing discovery: the pounds were actually coming off!''

One Saturday, excited over her weight loss, Barbara threw her old clothes out a second-story window in their home. Her daughter was in the front yard and saw the clothes flying out of the window. She cheered her mother with: ''It's raining fat clothes!''

I love my life!

Two years later, Barbara is trim and attractive on the outside, full of poise, warmth and self-confidence on the inside. Her cancer is in remission and she feels good. Now she exclaims, ''I love my life! I'm at my goal weight and I have a whole new life. The changes in my body are the most obvious thing that's happened to me. But even more important is the change in my attitude about myself. That has affected not only my weight, but my work as well.

BARBARA'S SUCCESS STORY (continued)

''I always thought I was an excellent administrator. I did everything I was supposed to do. But I didn't think my boss liked me all that much. I wasn't happy in my job.

''With my new self-confidence, I had an honest talk with my boss and learned he had requested me for the job because he liked my work. I was amazed. I thought he preferred someone else! How senseless to have gone all those months thinking he didn't want me!

''Since then, things have gone better in all areas of my life. My boss has given me more responsibility and extra projects. I've received $2,000 in accomplishment awards in the last six months.''

Feeling Good About Yourself

''I've learned that when you feel good about yourself, it affects every area of your life. I don't tell mean jokes about myself anymore. Now they're on the positive side, like: 'When I'm a millionaire, I'll buy the biggest house in town.' Your mind registers what you verbalize as fact. That's why I'm still doing my cards every day. Here are some of them:

- I see myself—from the inside out—at my goal weight.
- I am happy.
- I love my job.
- I have a wonderful working relationship with my boss.
- I am financially independent.
- I enjoy my co-workers.
- I exercise daily.
- I'm a worthwhile person with great ideas.
- I forgive my ex-husband.
- I wear makeup and fix my hair every day.
- I read a chapter in the Bible every day.
- I always eat healthy foods.
- I know I can, I know I can, I know I can.

"But here's one of my best cards," Barbara declared. "I wrote it last year:

> 'I have a wonderful, exciting social life with a kind, gentle, affectionate Christian man.'"

If you ask Barbara if reinforcements work, she gives you a knowing smile. "You tell me," she replies. "I got married two weeks ago. You guessed it. To a kind, gentle, affectionate Christian man.

Your Success Story

If you had a chance to talk with Barbara in person, what would you say to her?

_____

_____

Which success principles in Barbara's story do you see? (For example, "Keep on using a good process for 60 days even if you don't see the results immediately.")

_____

_____

_____

Barbara pictured herself accomplishing *her objectives, her pictures of excellence.* For example:

- I see myself at my goal weight wearing a size 7 red dress.

She also pictured herself using the practical, supporting processes that would help her reach her goal.

- I see my hand reaching into the refrigerator and picking up a handful of raw vegetables.
- I see myself on Saturday morning preparing a big container of raw veggies to have as snacks for the week.
- I see myself walking around the track four miles a day.

YOUR SUCCESS STORY (continued)

Picture Plus Supporting Processes

What is other example of a picture—and supporting process—that someone might use?

Word picture: _____

_____

Supporting process: _____

_____

When *you* accomplish *your dreams* like Barbara did, specifically what will you be seeing? In other words, describe one of your pictures of excellence.

_____

_____

What are some supporting processes you can put into your reinforcements to help you accomplish your picture?

_____

_____

Some of the reinforcements Barbara wrote were uncomfortable for her. For example, she wrote, ''I see myself at my goal weight wearing a size 7 red dress. I am a 120-pound woman.'' She reflected, ''Those reinforcements contrasted so wildly with the way I really lived that I could hardly bring myself to read those cards.''

What are the advantages to you of writing a word picture that stretches you beyond your comfort level?

_____

_____

Success stories always embody stretching and improving. And success stories add to your energy and persistence in pursuing your own happy endings.

SECTION WRAP-UP

To help you build your pattern of persistence, check the ideas from this section that have the most value for you:

☐ When I fill my mind with positive reinforcements, my behavior will gradually change to reflect what my mind believes to be true.

☐ I write and read my reinforcements even if I am not comfortable with what they say, because I know they represent self-fulfilling prophecies.

☐ I verbalize only the beliefs that will draw me forward instead of making mean jokes about my defects.

☐ I not only imagine pictures of excellence; I also imagine practical, supporting processes that will help me reach my targets

☐ I am a person of persistence, because I know that persistence is the key to making the improvements I want.

In the next section, you will explore how you can enjoy this same powerful process in just seven days.

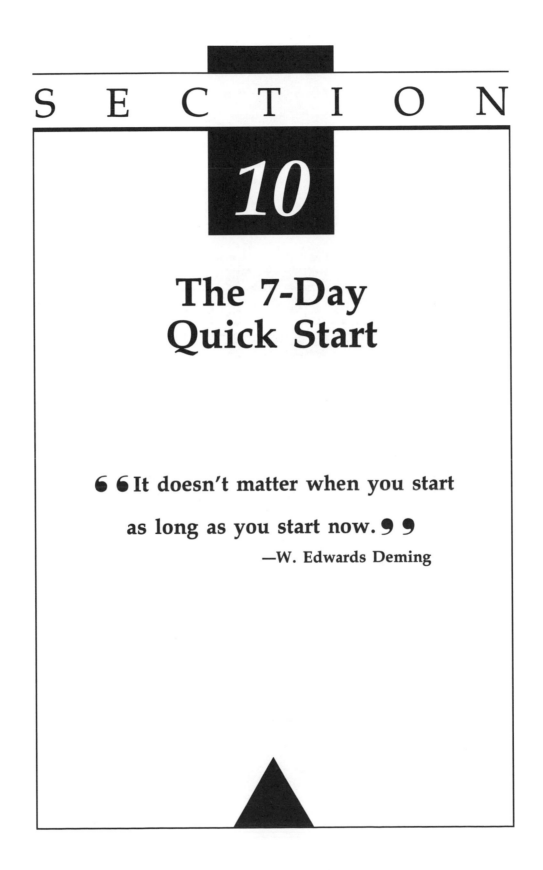

SECTION

10

The 7-Day
Quick Start

"It doesn't matter when you start as long as you start now."
—W. Edwards Deming

SUCCESS SECRET

Do it anyway.

It is better to improve along the
way than it is to perfect and delay.

7-DAY QUICK START—SHORTCUT TO SUCCESS

Here is how a group of seminar participants, both men and women, described their experiments with the 7-Day Quick-Start process:

> "It felt good even the first time."
> "I was surprised that something so simple works so well."
> "I did it in my car."
> "I did it in bed."
> "I did it faithfully for 39 days and nothing happened. Then on the 40th day . . ."
> "I only had 45 seconds of them and even that made a difference."
> "You guys, this is hot. Do it."

You can enjoy these same results. The Quick-Start experiment takes only two minutes, twice a day. Plus, you can do it anywhere.

► It helps you to experience, not just hear, how easy it is to benefit from purposeful self-talk (reinforcements).

► It is simple, quick and powerful.

You simply read a short collection of self-talk reinforcements. These statements have been researched and proven. Over the past decade, they have been used by hundreds of seminar participants. They work.

Two Minutes Morning and Evening

Consider this exercise a gift to yourself. As you start, keep your collection of self-talk statements to less than two minutes. If you select more than two minutes of reinforcements, it is tempting to push them aside.

Invest those two minutes in yourself the first thing in the morning and the last thing at night. Many people are the most receptive just before fully waking and before going to sleep. However, you can read your reinforcements during the day at any two times and still get good results. Read the reinforcements out loud for maximum benefit. The more of your senses you involve in your learning, the more value you will receive.

Each time you read your reinforcements, reward yourself by marking a star or check mark on your daily calendar. You may be surprised how a simple reward system motivates. In some ways, most of us are children at heart, enjoying the fun of earning stars. Use any simple reward system that works for you.

SUCCESS TIPS

The Place

The 7-Day Quick Start works the best when you anchor this new habit to a place or an activity that you already do each day. Some people read their reinforcements in bed after they wake up and again before going to sleep. Others read them while brushing their teeth, morning and evening. Others read while riding in the car pool back and forth to work. Still others review their reinforcements while drinking a cup of coffee after breakfast and dinner. Your creativity will lead you to the way to link your reinforcements to your daily patterns.

Doing It Anyway

Since the following list of reinforcements takes only two minutes to read, you can read them all, or you can pick the ones that especially apply to you.

Some people feel guilty the first time they read these reinforcements. They know the ideas already, and they also know they have not been fully implementing them. If you are one of those people, forgive yourself and keep moving forward. Some people feel guilty if they miss a time. If you do, you can make it up the next day. You will soon replace any guilt with satisfaction and accomplishment.

You may want to put your reinforcements on three-by-five cards. Writing one idea to a card makes them easy to update. If you do not have cards handy, you can read the list out of this book. Whatever you do, now is a great time to *do it anyway*.

Making It Easy for Yourself

At the beginning of the collection of reinforcements, you will see five with a star in front. These are specially designed to keep your reinforcement system going. They put gas in the tank. You will get better, more consistent results when you include them *each* time you read your reinforcements.

INVESTING IN YOURSELF FOR SEVEN MORE DAYS

After the first seven days, invest in yourself again. The first exhilarating taste makes it easier for you to do it for another week. As you go along, ideas for refining your reinforcements will occur to you. Add them. Take out the ones you no longer want. Make this an on-going process of self-talk and self-coaching that will enable you to enjoy more satisfaction and add more value.

The 60-Day Guarantee

Since people who are feeling stress often say that sixty days is too long of a commitment, planning for seven days at a time works well. The most power and best results come from using your reinforcements for sixty days. With the hundreds of people in seminars who used the reinforcements, there was a 95 percent success rate for those who invested two minutes, morning and evening, for sixty days. They gained the improvements they wanted.

The secret: **The Right Reinforcements plus Consistency**
2 + 2 × 60 = Less Stress, More Motivation
and Better Results

Dru Scott Quick-Start Set of Reinforcements

To keep the reinforcements going:

- I listen to my reinforcements twice a day. It is a great way to reduce stress, feel more energized, and accomplish the right things.

- I read my reinforcements cards out loud to myself the last thing at night and the first in the morning.

- I put together pictures of excellence and processes to get there.

- It's fun to figure out the wording and word pictures that work best for me.

- I get a kick out of marking a check or a star on my calendar every time I read my reinforcements.

To build motivation:

- I picture what I want in wonderful detail, because pictures add to my drive and discipline.

- There is always something I can do.

- I always have choices.

- I turn problems into opportunities, so I am always in a good mood.

- I focus and I finish.

At a time of stress, I picture a baseball diamond:

- At first base, I relax and breathe deeply for a couple of minutes.

- At second base, I accept my feelings and the realities of my current situation.

- At third base, I picture how I want the situation to be.

- At home base, I take some action toward the solution I want or toward containing or mastering the situation. I feel relief when I take purposeful action.

To keep my energy level high:

- I Grab 15. It is incredible how much I can accomplish in fifteen minutes.

- No temporary parking spots. I put it in place or in use.

- My feelings make me human.

- My customers are always happy to hear from me because I help them get what they want.

- I add value.

To build teamwork and relationships:

- I forgive and I feel free.

- If I have a difficult person in my life, I fix my part of the problem.

- I help put together mutually satisfying solutions. Win-win does work the best!

- I ask for what I want.

- I prevent problems.

- I fix the process and not the person.

To enjoy today:

- This is a great day.

- I have a big smile as I exercise. After just thirty minutes I feel so much energy.

- My Quiet Time is the high point of my day.

- I never have a dull moment because I am always working to check off accomplishments on my weekly target sheet.

- I give myself a great start because I wrap up the tough top priority first.

- I do it anyway.

- I do it now!

(You have special permission to reproduce the Dru Scott Quick-Start Reinforcements for your own use at no additional charge when you purchase this book.)

SECTION WRAP-UP

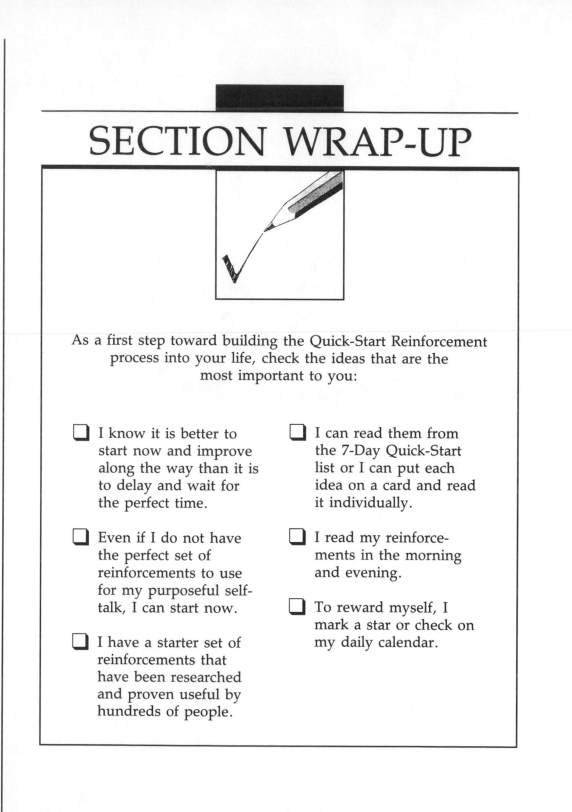

As a first step toward building the Quick-Start Reinforcement process into your life, check the ideas that are the most important to you:

❏ I know it is better to start now and improve along the way than it is to delay and wait for the perfect time.

❏ Even if I do not have the perfect set of reinforcements to use for my purposeful self-talk, I can start now.

❏ I have a starter set of reinforcements that have been researched and proven useful by hundreds of people.

❏ I can read them from the 7-Day Quick-Start list or I can put each idea on a card and read it individually.

❏ I read my reinforcements in the morning and evening.

❏ To reward myself, I mark a star or check on my daily calendar.

Enjoy Continuous Improvement

Stress That Motivates
Self-Talk Secrets for Success

It forms how you feel.
It directs what you do.
It shapes what you earn.

Yet it:
Costs only pennies,
Takes only minutes.

And it
Is one of those things in life
that is totally within your control.

It is
what you say to yourself.
It is particularly
what you say to yourself over and over,
Your mental background music.

So fill your mind with the music that
Encourages you,
Directs you
and
Inspires you.

Invest two minutes each morning and evening
in purposeful self-talk—your reinforcements.

ACKNOWLEGMENTS

The participants in my seminars and speeches—for all that they have taught me.

Al Beller, my first manager in a career job—for telling me years ago: ''Dru, rather than concentrating on things you can't change, accept them. Work on things you can change, and by all means, change what you say to yourself.

Bert Decker, my husband—for being such an inspiration to me; and for my new family Allison, Sam and Ben—for calling me to grow and be my best.

DuPont—for funding the research and seminars behind much of this book. What a privilege to work with an organization so committed to people and continuous improvement.

Barbara Latta—for her inspiring story.

Mike Crisp—for being such a visionary in publishing.

Frank Nuessle, Crisp Publications—for dreaming up title #89—*Stress That Motivates: Self-Talk Secrets for Success.* As soon as he said it, we all agreed ''Yes, this is it!''

Kathleen Barcos—for her grace in juggling all the pieces that fall into the hands of an executive editor.

Carol Gift Page and Jim Denney—for being such great trainers on putting life into writing.

For the people who have added so much to me and this book: Lenora Borecek, Robert Bronzan, Ph.D., Mary Butler, Lowell Dicke, Peter Drucker, Stephen DeVeber, Bill Kirkey, Claire Lee, Lenora Leffert, Dave English, Jane Janson, Stephen Karpman, M.D., Elizabeth Paeth Lasker, M.D., Kris Poggioli and Mahlia Riebeling.

NOTES

NOTES

NOTES

NOTES

NOTES

NOW AVAILABLE FROM CRISP PUBLICATIONS

Books • Videos • CD Roms • Computer-Based Training Products

If you enjoyed this book, we have great news for you. There are over 200 books available in the *50-Minute*™ Series. To request a free full-line catalog, contact your local distributor or Crisp Publications, Inc., 1200 Hamilton Court, Menlo Park, CA 94025. Our toll-free number is 800-422-7477.

Subject Areas Include:

Management
Human Resources
Communication Skills
Personal Development
Marketing/Sales
Organizational Development
Customer Service/Quality
Computer Skills
Small Business and Entrepreneurship
Adult Literacy and Learning
Life Planning and Retirement

CRISP WORLDWIDE DISTRIBUTION

English language books are distributed worldwide. Major international distributors include:

ASIA/PACIFIC

Australia/New Zealand: In Learning, PO Box 1051 Springwood QLD, Brisbane, Australia 4127
Telephone: 7-841-1061, Facsimile: 7-841-1580
ATTN: Mssrs. Gordon

Singapore: Graham Brash (Pvt) Ltd. 32, Gul Drive, Singapore 2262
Telphone: 65-861-1336, Facsimile: 65-861-4815
ATTN: Mr. Campbell

EUROPEAN UNION

England: Flex Training, Ltd. 9-15 Hitchin Street, Baldock, Hertfordshire, SG7 6AL
Telephone: 1-462-896000, Facsimile: 1-462-892417
ATTN: Mr. Willets

INDIA

Multi-Media HRD, Pvt., Ltd., National House, Tulloch Road, Appolo Bunder, Bombay, India 400-039
Telephone: 91-22-204-2281, Facsimile: 91-22-283-6478
ATTN: Mssrs. Aggarwal

MIDDLE EAST

United Arab Emirates: Al-Mutanabbi Bookshop, PO Box 71946, Abu Dhabi
Telephone: 971-2-321-519, Facsimile: 971-2-317-706

NORTH AMERICA

Canada: Reid Publishing, Ltd., Box 69559-109 Thomas Street, Oakville, Ontario Canada L6J 7R4.
Telephone: (905) 842-4428, Facsimile: (905) 842-9327

SOUTH AMERICA

Mexico: Grupo Editorial Iberoamerica, Serapio Rendon #125, Col. San Rafael, 06470 Mexico, D.F.
Telephone: 525-705-0585, Facsimile: 525-535-2009
ATTN: Señor Grepe

SOUTH AFRICA

Alternative Books, Unit A3 Sanlam Micro Industrial Park, Hammer Avenue STRYDOM Park, Randburg, 2194 South Africa
Telephone: 2711 792 7730, Facsimile: 2711 792 7787
ATTN: Mr. de Haas

Selected Crisp titles are available in 23 languages. For more information contact International Publishing Manager, Suzanne Kelly-Lyall at (415) 323-6100.